Bottom-Line Business Writing

BOTTOM-LINE BUSINESS WRITING

John S. Fielden
Ronald E. Dulek

Prentice-Hall, Inc., Englewood Cliffs, New Jersey

Prentice-Hall International, Inc., *London*
Prentice-Hall of Australia, Pty. Ltd., *Sydney*
Prentice-Hall Canada, Inc., *Toronto*
Prentice-Hall of India Private Ltd., *New Delhi*
Prentice-Hall of Japan, Inc., *Tokyo*
Prentice-Hall of Southeast Asia Pte. Ltd., *Singapore*
Whitehall Books, Ltd., Wellington, *New Zealand*
Editora Prentice-Hall do Brasil Ltda., *Rio de Janeiro*

© 1984 by

PRENTICE-HALL, INC.

Englewood Cliffs, N.J.

Library of Congress Cataloging in Publication Data

Fielden, John S.
  Bottom-line business writing.

  Includes index.
  1. Business report writing. 2. Memorandums.
3. Commercial correspondence. I. Dulek, Ronald E.
II. Title.
HF5719.F53   1983   658.4'53   83-19192
ISBN 0-13-080283-2

Printed in the United States of America

THE AUTHORS

John S. Fielden, Ph.D., University Professor of Management Communications, University of Alabama, is the author of nine *Harvard Business Review* articles, including the all-time *Harvard Business Review* classic, "What Do You Mean I Can't Write?" A consultant to IBM since 1964, Dr. Fielden is formerly Dean of the Business Schools of Boston University and the University of Alabama. He is a writing consultant to General Electric, Dun and Bradstreet, General Foods and other U.S. and Canadian firms.

Ronald E. Dulek, Ph.D., is Associate Professor and Coordinator of Management Communications at the University of Alabama. He is consultant to IBM, OSHA, the United States Department of Health and Human Services, AT&T, and other public and private organizations. His articles on business communications have been published in *Business Horizons, Journal of Business Communications, Personnel Journal, Personnel* magazine, and *IEEE Transactions on Professional Communications*.

DEDICATION

To Sally, Daniel, Laura and Jean

ACKNOWLEDGMENTS

We wish to acknowledge the valuable contributions made to the development of materials in this book by Robert Yellowlees, President, American Telesystems Corporation, and by William F. Speights, Alexander Saliby Jr., Joseph W. Piech, William Blashke, all of the National Marketing Division of IBM.

THE PERSONAL
AND CORPORATE BENEFITS
OF BOTTOM-LINE WRITING

This is a book on writing to get a job done, to complete a transaction. It is intended to enable you to write the way successful executives do. The book is based on twenty-five years of working with top executives, closely observing (a) how they express themselves and (b) how they expect others to write to them.

What you write is your calling card. It represents you. It tells people how you value their time and yours. What kind of representation do you want? Let's try a few analogies:

Golf. Do you want to write like a golfer who whacks the ball from rough to tree to bunker before getting even close to the hole—and then three putts?

Football. Do you want to be a runner who fumbles the ball around in his own backfield rather than rushing toward the goal line?

Basketball. Do you want to be a player who never scores because he is always dribbling the ball around at midcourt?

These are the ways many people in business actually write. The purpose of this book is to help you to be a golfer who is always driving the ball toward the hole, not the woods—a football player who runs only north and south toward the goal line—a basketball player who always drives for the basket. We call this kind of effort *bottom-line* writing.

The book is based on a series of thirteen bottom-line rules, with very sparse explanations of these principles. We do not believe in long books. We believe people learn to write by practice, not by being talked into becoming better writers.

This text is organized into four parts:

- Part I presents eight bottom-line rules to apply when writing messages that convey nonsensitive information.
- Part II presents five bottom-line rules to apply when writing sensitive messages where bottom-lining may or may not be wise or appropriate.
- Part III offers readers an opportunity to interact with the text and hone their skills at identifying, placing, and writing bottom-line sentences.
- Finally, part IV shows you how to construct a bottom-line clinic within your office or corporation so that you can take effective, practical steps toward combating wasted time within your organization.

Why does anyone need to learn to be a bottom-line writer? What's in it for you, personally? And what's in it for your organization?

PERSONAL BENEFITS

We cannot guarantee that bottom-line writing will speed your climb up the corporate ladder. We do, however, know from examinations of memos written by high-level corporate executives that these executives usually are excellent bottom-line writers.

Did they get to the top because they bottom-lined their communications? We don't know. But somewhere in their corporate careers these executives discovered that writing in a namby-pamby, beat-around-the-bush organizational pattern is fine for college writing courses, but it doesn't help your progress within a corporation. These executives adopted a method of presenting their thoughts directly, efficiently, and effectively. This is the method this book teaches you.

BENEFITS TO YOUR COMPANY OR GROUP

While you are helped as an individual to communicate in a clear, efficient manner, your organization will discover a significant drop in on-the-job time spent in the communication process. Writing and reading time will decrease and a significant dollar savings will result. This will happen if not only you, but everybody in your organization converts to bottom-line reporting.

One large international corporation we work with estimated some years ago that the average cost for every memo or letter written in that corporation was more than ten dollars. One division of this same corporation monitored the number of documents sent out by its divisional headquarters staff and found that the number exceeded 9 million pieces in one year. Admittedly, some were multiple copies (in some instances thousands of duplicate messages were sent). So let's assume only 10% of these 9 million letters and memos were individually composed. Even so, the cost of writing just these letters was 9 million dollars.

Yet, the cost of writing is only part of the picture. The cost of reading what is written is significantly greater. One large organization recently discovered through internal analysis that its professional staff members spend an average of 58 percent of their time reading and writing! No wonder experts estimate that American industry spent over $1 billion in reading time in 1981. Imagine the savings by reducing this time by 10, 20, or even 30 percent. That's what bottom-line reporting can do.

And these benefits are now yours, thanks to *Bottom-Line Business Writing*.

John S. Fielden
Ronald E. Dulek

We have made every effort to avoid sexist language in this text. In situations where a designation is necessary, such as in various scenarios, we have alternated male and female names.

CONTENTS

Introduction: The Personal and Corporate Benefits of Bottom-Line Writing 5

Personal Benefits • Benefits to Your Company or Group

I: HOW TO BOTTOM-LINE NONSENSITIVE MESSAGES 15

1. Bottom-Lining Your Way to Direct, Efficient Memos ... 17
   Non-Bottom-Lined Messages Are Wasting Your Time

2: Bottom-Line Nonsensitive Messages to Save Your Readers' Time 21

3: Three Assumptions to Avoid When Writing a Bottom-Line Message 24

4: Two Rules to Keep You from Backsliding into Non-Bottom-Line Ways 28

5: Three More Rules to Keep You from Backsliding 35

6: Lead Your Reader by the Nose Through Complex Communications 41

II: WHEN AND WHEN NOT TO BOTTOM-LINE SENSITIVE MESSAGES **47**

7: Consider Relationship, Position, and the Message 49

8: Four Sensitive Messages You Can Bottom-Line
Efficiency 51
Bottom-Line Positive Messages • Positive Persuasive
Requests • Blind Persuasive Situations • Negative Message
Downward

9: Two Sensitive Messages You Should Think Twice
About Before Bottom-Lining 60
Negative Messages Upward • Negative Persuasive
Messages

III: MASTERING THE MIND-SET OF BOTTOM-LINE WRITING **71**

10: Use the "So What?" Factor to Recognize
Bottom-Line Sentences 73
Recognizing a Bottom-Line Sentence • Finding the
Bottom Line in Longer Passages • Develop the Bottom-
Line Habit for Efficiency

11: How to Write Acceptable First-Draft Bottom-Line
Messages 83
How to Write Successful First Drafts in Psychologically
Sensitive Situations • Writing Down with Sensitivity

IV: ESTABLISHING A BOTTOM-LINE CLINIC TO SAVE YOUR TIME AND YOUR COMPANY'S MONEY **95**

12: Guidelines for Your Own Bottom-Line Clinic 97
Spread the Bottom-Line Word Through a Bottom-Line
Clinic • What You Need to Operate the Clinic • Clinic
Wrapup • Insecurity Masquerading as Thoroughness •
Review of Bottom-Line Rules

Appendix Illustrations **104**

Appendix A: Bottom-Line Illustrations **105**

How to Bottom-Line Informational Messages • How to
Bottom-Line Positive Messages • How to Bottom-Line
Negative Messages • How to Bottom-Line Persuasive
Messages

Appendix B: Circuitous Illustrations **136**

Circuitous Persuasive Messages • Circuitous Negative
Messages

Index **151**

HOW TO BOTTOM-LINE NONSENSITIVE MESSAGES

1

BOTTOM-LINING YOUR WAY
TO DIRECT, EFFICIENT MEMOS

We estimate that 95 percent of all the writing that most businesspeople do is not particularly sensitive, at least not in the "hot potato" sense. Therefore, unless you have an unusual job (such as answering complaint letters, handling claims and adjustments, or dealing with stockholders), there is little need to beat around the bush and fail to bottom-line your messages.

This section of our book tells you how to organize nonsensitive messages that tell readers everything they need to know in the most direct, efficient fashion possible—unless there is a *very* good reason not to do so.

If you want to be this kind of writer, we guarantee that your approach to your own writing will change dramatically as you read this book. In addition, what you demand from others who write to you or who write letters for your signature will also change. You and they will never get over this book's message.

The book's simple message is that you should bottom-line almost everything you write. That is, tell your readers what's at the bottom line of your communication. Tell them:

1. Why you are writing to them,
2. What your purpose is,
3. What you want them to do,

And most of the time, do so immediately, in the first few sentences. Sounds simple, doesn't it? Surely every businessperson should do this every time he or she writes, but that is not the case. Just let us show you **what** bottom-line reporting is really all about. Then we'll ask you to take a good hard look at some of your own memos and letters. See for yourself.

NON-BOTTOM-LINED MESSAGES ARE WASTING YOUR TIME!

Nonsensitive messages that don't tell immediately what their bottom line is waste a busy reader's time and patience. See how you react to the following real-life memos (disguised, of course) that are typical of those you see every day on the job.

Memo A

TO: Frank Finnegan, President

FROM: T.R. Little

SUBJECT: Manufacturing Plan Review

As you know, I have been asked to chair the Manufacturing Plan Review effort. You have stated regularly that this planning effort should receive top priority.

I propose that we should hold preplanning meetings at various company sites:

• In Gastonville, July 1.
• In Charlottesburg, July 5.
• In Durbin, July 10.

At these meetings, I would like all plant managers to discuss their views on:

1. Retooling progress for new products under development at each site.
2. Any needed extra financing for problems encountered in retooling.
3. Adequacy of each site's managerial structure and organization.
4. Input they would like to make to next year's manufacturing plan.

These discussions should establish production schedules for all of our new and existing products that complement our marketing strategy. I also intend to reassess our manufacturing organization and its effectiveness for Mike Montani.

How did you react to this memo? Although the memo is visually attractive, didn't you find that you were jumping back and forth from itemized information in search of a bottom line? And were you able to process mentally the information you were reading?

Memo B

TO: Frank Finnegan

FROM: G. H. Conrad

SUBJECT: Consolidation of Marketing Functions in New Office Facilities

I am working with our organization department on consolidating headquarters marketing functions into the new building at Pebble Brook. The new building will be ready for occupancy in September.

I suggest that we leave Market Research in its current location but provide it with additional space for expansion. I also recommend the following occupancy plan for the Pebble Brook building:

1. Consolidate all of the Marketing Communications people into this new building.
2. Relocate our Advertising and Media people from Northside to this new building.
3. Centralize the Procurement function entirely in the new building.

These moves will consolidate all of headquarters Marketing into the Pebble Brook location with the exception of Ron Reynolds and his Marketing Research people. They will remain in building I because of their heavy utilization of our computer facilities.

I have attached a preliminary building layout, floor by floor. Please let me know if you agree with this plan.

How did you react to this memo? Did you scan the memo looking for the bottom line?

You probably agree that both memos are typical of what you see every day on the job. You also probably agree that they are wasteful and needlessly discursive.

Check up on what we're saying. See if it's true about writers in your organization. Pick up any group of letters or memos that you've just received. Don't choose one- or two-sentence notes; focus on those that cover at least a page to a page and a half. Read the first one or two paragraphs of each of these memos.

After reading these paragraphs, did you find yourself mentally asking the writer, "So what? Why are you telling me this? What's your purpose?" If so, you are reading memos that have not been bottom-lined, memos that force you to wade through potentially useless information to find out what all of it has to do with you.

How adequate was your sample? Check further. Scrutinize more memos. Make sure they come from a wide range of authors. If you find more than 10 percent that tell the writer's purpose in the first paragraph, you will be lucky and we will be astounded.

Here's another challenge. Examine some of your own memos. See how effectively *you* bottom-line your purpose for writing. Could it be that you could become more efficient, too?

If so, ask yourself this: Is it right to make others suffer the way they do you? Think of the frustration you feel every day when you pore over one-and-one-half-, two-, or three-page memos only to find at the very end that they have little or no relevance to you. In essence, you don't even know why these memos were sent to you in the first place.

Or, remember how you felt the last time you struggled diligently through an obscure technical memo, only to discover at the very end that this information was actually very important to you? Then, you had to reread the entire document. If the writer had let you know at the beginning what he or she was talking about—and why you should read the memo—you could have possibly read the document once and been done with it.

If you and your colleagues don't like to read inefficiently organized memos, then don't write memos organized in this way. This situation resembles an old joke: A man, flexing his arm, says to the doctor, "It hurts when I do this." The doctor replies, "Then don't *do* that! Twenty dollars please."

If the whole business world would start bottom-lining at once, we would all save a great deal of time and money.

2

BOTTOM-LINE NONSENSITIVE MESSAGES TO SAVE YOUR READERS' TIME

Wouldn't it be nice if people sent memos as bottom-lined as the following revisions of the opening paragraphs of memos A and B in section 1?

Memo A—Bottom-Lined

TO: Frank Finnegan, President

FROM: T. R. Little

SUBJECT: Manufacturing Plan Review

This memo is to inform you of the details of our manufacturing review meetings, should these be of interest to you. In brief, the purposes of these discussions are:

    A. To establish production schedules for all of our new and existing products that complement our marketing strategy.

    B. To reassess our manufacturing organization and its effectiveness for Mike Montani.

Here are the details:

_____

_____

If you are Finnegan and these manufacturing review meetings are not of interest to you, then you have the choice of not wasting your time by reading further. You, the reader, would be in control of your time, not the writer.

Memo B—Bottom-Lined

TO:　　　Frank Finnegan

FROM:　　G. H. Conrad

SUBJECT: Consolidation of Marketing Functions

Please review the attached occupancy plan for the Pebble Brook building and let me know if you agree with it.

As you will see, this plan consolidates all of headquarters Marketing (with the exception of Market Research) into our new building.

We will begin occupancy in September.

Now that you know that you are being asked to agree or disagree with this office arrangement in the new building, you are alerted to read the attached plan carefully. These revisions exemplify the first of our bottom-line rules, which, if followed, will invariably lead you to effective bottom-lined messages.

```
BOTTOM-LINE RULE 1: STATE YOUR PURPOSE FIRST UN-
                    LESS THERE ARE OVERRIDING
                    REASONS FOR NOT DOING SO.
```

This rule is simple enough, yet 90 percent or more of the memos and reports that simply convey factual information break this rule. In symbolic form, here's what most three-page corporate memo reports look like:

Page 1:　　Theodore Roosevelt
　　　　　　John Kennedy
　　　　　　Millard Fillmore

Page 2:   Abraham Lincoln
          Lyndon Johnson
          George Washington
          Andrew Jackson
Page 3:   Dwight Eisenhower
          James Buchanan
          William Harrison

"Wait a minute," you say after reading the list. "Why is all this being sent to me?" Usually, it's the final sentence of most memos that tells you:

> I thought you would like to see a list of presidents arranged according to their age at inauguration.

"Who cares about the ages of presidents at inauguration?" you cry. "Why tell me all that stuff?"

"Ha! Ha!" says the writer. "I made you read what I was interested in, didn't I?"

The point is obvious. *If writers state their purpose at the beginning, readers can immediately decide whether or not to read the message.* And lots of writers selfishly don't want to give the reader the choice. As a result, readers are forced to read the equivalent of our symbolic list of presidents—until they are let in on the secret at the end. Only then do they know that they didn't want to read the useless information in the first place.

Of course, by stating their purpose first in a memo, writers run the risk that busy readers won't read all that they've written. But is a well-run organization being operated for the pleasure of time-wasters? We hope not.

3

THREE ASSUMPTIONS TO AVOID WHEN WRITING A BOTTOM-LINE MESSAGE

The notion of stating the purpose first appeals to a wide variety of business readers, especially when it saves them from the drudgery of having to wade through entire memos in search of a one-sentence purpose. Why, then, are purposes so rarely put at the beginning? There are three reasons:

1. Writers assume readers know the purpose, don't state it, and force readers to infer what a message is really about.
2. Writers frequently convince themselves that, since they have told the reader the subject of the message, they have actually told their purpose in writing. Subject and purpose are usually not the same.
3. Most people don't know what they really want to say until after they've written it.

Let's take a close look at these reasons so that we can appreciate and overcome the faulty assumptions on which each is based.

1. Writers Assume That Readers Know the Purpose

Writers, being tremendously involved in their own work, often assume that their readers are equally knowledgeable about its importance and relevance. Furthermore, writers assume that readers are able (and eager) to infer the writer's purpose in communicating. Imagine that you are sitting in your office on Monday morning and the mail arrives. You look at the first memo. It says, in three paragraphs, "Joan Brown passed her Certified Management Accountant examination."

"That's nice," you think, "but so what? Why are you telling me this?" Obviously, the writer felt that this information was important to you, but its importance completely escapes you. Either you throw the memo in the wastebasket or you write back and say, "Why did you tell me that Joan Brown passed her CMA exam?"

If the writer had taken into consideration his or her purpose in writing you, the memo might have read something like this:

> You asked me to let you know when Joan Brown completed her CMA exam so that you can support the promotion I committed.
>
> I am happy to tell you that Joan passed the exam with high grades. Therefore, I'd appreciate your writing an appropriate letter to recommend her promotion.

"Oh," you say, "That's right! I did promise. All right, I'll recommend Brown's promotion."

2. Writers Frequently Convince Themselves That, Since They Have Told the Reader the Subject of the Message, They Have Actually Told Their Purpose in Writing

There is a marked difference between a subject and a purpose. That is why subject lines in reports and memos usually don't do the job. They are, for the most part, key words to use in filing documents. For example, one writer relied on this subject line in his memo:

Subject: Route 128

Imagine you've received this memo. What does "Route 128" mean to you? You need a first paragraph statement of purpose, like this:

> For your information, Route 128 has been eliminated by our real estate people and is no longer a potential site for the New England Headquarters building.

Let's look at another instance. A writer stated in an opening paragraph:

> I am quite interested in the revenue contribution made by the marketing support system Fred and Mary have been working on. Their system has evolved since they joined ABCD ...."

The writer obviously thought the message did its job by stating promptly the subject to be discussed. But you wonder, "So *you* are interested. So what? What's this got to do with me?" It would have been far more effective if the writer had made the purpose clear, like this:

> I would very much appreciate your authorizing an independent evaluation of the revenue contributions made by the marketing support system that Fred and Mary have been working on. I think you will find the results as interesting as I will.

"Okay," says the reader. "Tell me about it." The statement of purpose has set the stage for meaningful communication.

3. Most People Don't Know What They Really Want to Say Until After They've Written It

In almost everything writers have written—all their lives—they have inscribed a history of their thoughts on paper as they worked their way through a problem. (In many cases, they don't know what they think until after they're through writing.)

Here is an outline of the way almost everyone's mind operates. Let's pose a question: "Should we do business with Smith and Brown?" After thinking, the average person writes a memo organized around these key thoughts:

- "The question under consideration is whether we should do business with Smith and Brown."
- "There are certain benefits to dealing with Smith and Brown."
- "There are certain disadvantages."
- "After weighing each, I conclude that the disadvantages outweigh the advantages."
- "Therefore, we should not do business with Smith and Brown."

What you've got to ask yourself is this: As a reader, what information do you want to receive? And in what order? Don't you want the bottom line first? Giving you that bottom line should be the writer's purpose, and it should be stated first:

I recommend that we not do business with Smith and Brown. Here are my reasons:

1. _____
2. _____
3. _____

Appendix A contains a detailed analysis should you require it.

Obviously, this memo is not an outline of the way our minds worked as we analyzed the problem. But do we really need to give the reader a blow-by-blow account of our thoughts as we worked our way to a conclusion? Shouldn't we give the reader our conclusions first? Isn't transmitting those conclusions our real purpose in writing? Shouldn't the justification (or defense) of our conclusion follow—not precede—our recommendation?

Businesspeople must learn to think things through first, before writing a final draft. Then, once they know the bottom line ("We should not do business with Smith and Brown"), they should move that bottom-line conclusion to the beginning of their communication.

4

TWO RULES TO KEEP YOU FROM BACKSLIDING INTO NON-BOTTOM-LINE WAYS

Let's assume you are cured, at least partially, of the plague of not bottom-lining your purpose. Will you now experience backsliding? You'll have to watch yourself like a hawk. There are four evidences of relapse that you will have to keep an eye on. Here are the first two:

Relapse 1: Bottom-lining only one of your purposes for writing and burying the other.

Relapse 2: Assuming that your readers always need a background briefing (whether they do or not) before you let them know your purpose for writing. (This assumption conveniently allows you to ignore bottom-line rule 1.)

To help you cope with these backsliding tendencies, we present two more valuable bottom-line rules.

BOTTOM-LINE RULE 2: IF THERE IS MORE THAN ONE PURPOSE TO A COMMUNICATION, STATE BOTH PURPOSES AT THE BEGINNING, OR WRITE TWO MEMOS.

Do you ever have problems with people calling and saying, "I didn't realize you actually recommended that we take such-and-such an action?" or asking contentiously, "Why wasn't I informed that you planned to scrap the Higgins deal?" If so, perhaps closer adherence to bottom-line rule 2 will eliminate many of your problems.

If you have more than one purpose, don't bottom-line only one of them and bury the others. Face it; your readers do not like to read. The sooner they get through with a memo or letter, the better they like it.

Don't we all begin reading in hopes of deciphering a message's purpose and then quickly disposing of it? And once we think we've found that purpose, aren't we likely to stop reading? The majority of business readers we teach admit to doing exactly this.

If you look closely enough at the correspondence traveling around your company, you probably will find many examples of buried purposes. They arise because many writers are so poorly disciplined in their writing that around the middle of the third paragraph they say, "Oh, yes, I forgot to mention this, but I really think you ought to ...."

Think of how you read a memo. Once you spot certain key words, aren't you apt to stop reading? One key word is *recommendation*. Once you see a recommendation, aren't you tempted to stop reading at that point and focus on whether or not to accept the recommendation?

Memo D illustrates this tendency. In many ways, it is a good memo.

Memo D

TO: J. B. Alvarez

FROM: Susan Greenspan

Jim, I recommend that we reduce the purchase price of the F–62 line as soon as possible for the following reasons:
1. The entire line has had no significant ...,
2. Customer acceptances are off markedly ...,
3. We will not be able to achieve our ....

I understand that some of our manufacturers' reps have proposed bonuses or rebates to help move certain elements of the F–62 line. Also, some retailers are requesting that we reduce our down-payment requirement from 25 percent to 10 percent. I recommend that we aggressively support both of these proposals.

While our current sales plan has a 15 to 20 percent profit for F–62 products, I believe 10 percent is a more realistic figure since:
1. Our Commercial Analysis people believe ....
2. With lower prices, the F–62 line would be positioned ....

You will notice that the first recommendation is made clearly in the first paragraph. This is wonderful. But you can see how a reader would be fooled into thinking that this is the sole recommendation being made. As a result, this memo is not very clear or effective. In fact, it is deceptive.

You tend to think that just one recommendation is being made. But in the end of the last sentence in the second paragraph, there is a second recommendation bootlegged in. And this recommendation is just as important as the first. If busy readers read this memo the way they read most communications, they probably will miss the second recommendation.

Why accidentally fool your reader? This writer should have begun by stating that her purpose was to make two recommendations. Something like the following would have done the job!

Memo D—Bottom-Lined

TO: J. B. Alvarez

FROM: Susan Greenspan

I have two recommendations about the F–62 line. Specifically:
1. We should reduce the purchase price on the F–62 line as soon as possible because:
   A. The entire line has had no significant ....
   B. Customer acceptances are off markedly ....
   C. We will not be able to achieve our ....
2. We should aggressively support the following suggestions made by our manufacturing reps and our retailers for stimulating F–62 line sales:
   A. Some manufacturers' reps have proposed ....
   B. Some retailers are requesting ....

While our sales plan has a 15 to 20 percent profit for F–62 products, I believe ....

Another bottom-line rule to prevent backsliding is:

BOTTOM-LINE RULE 3: STATE YOUR PURPOSE FIRST, EVEN IF YOU KNOW YOUR READERS NEED A BRIEFING BEFORE THEY CAN FULLY UNDERSTAND THE PURPOSE OF YOUR COMMUNICATION.

This is perhaps the most difficult of the bottom-line reporting rules. There are so many reporting situations where writers feel exceedingly insecure about blurting out their purpose. Writers tend to feel they have to explain—especially when writing to a superior—why they are asking for something to be done. Let's make up a few typical situations where such is the case.

Suppose your company plans to raise prices on October 1. You want to urge your most important customers to place their orders before that date. But you do not know for certain whether they want to buy or not. You are afraid to bottom-line your purpose and begin your letter with, "Please get your order in before September 30." You are afraid of appearing too pushy.

You are also afraid to write, "Please get your order in before September 30 because we are going to raise our prices on October 1." Now your bottom-line sentence not only sounds pushy, but it also could easily be perceived as a threat.

Consequently, in situations like this, most writers start rehearsing the history of price changes in the recent past, leading up to the fact that there is going to be a price change on October 1. Only then do they feel safe enough to tell the readers that they had better get their orders in before September 30.

But why not follow Bottom-Line Rule 3? Why not begin with the real purpose? Is it better to beat around the bush and run the risk that your best customers, by refusing to wade through several paragraphs of apparent nonsense, will end up angry with you because you didn't warn them about the coming price rise?

Let's take another example. Suppose you want your superior to approve a transfer of salary funds from an unfilled position so that the money can be used to hire a temporary consultant needed for a certain task. Most writers would be afraid to bottom-line their request: "Please approve the hiring of a consultant to accomplish the planned departmental reorganization.

He or she could be compensated from unspent salary funds in budget line 4783."

Instead, most writers would begin by pointing out how understaffed their department is and how upsetting the proposed reorganization has been to many people. They might then consider several alternative courses of action that might be taken. And only after that might they dare to recommend hiring a consultant as the best available alternative.

But what's so bad about telling your boss forthrightly what you want? Is boring the boss to death the better alternative? Is defensively presenting all of your arguments before you even make the request any less risky than directly asking for what you need? Most people foolishly think so.

There are situations that call for you to pause and consider whether a background briefing of your reader is truly necessary. But the general insecurity of most people is such that they tend to conclude that just about every situation requires an introductory briefing, whether it really does or not.

For the sake of significant time-saving on the part of both superiors and subordinates, we suggest that bosses make bottom-line rule 3 mandatory for all subordinates. In this way, the subordinates are relieved of anxiety about whether it is wise or unwise to give a background briefing. To bottom-line a point is simply required.

Superiors should slam the door firmly on subordinates' strong tendencies to regard every memo situation as requiring a background briefing. A smart boss will say:

> You tell me first why you are writing to me, what your purpose is, and what you want me to do. Then offer your background briefing. If I need the briefing, I'll read it. If I don't, I won't. At least this way I'll know what you're talking about right away. This way we'll both save time.

Here is an actual memo that affords a classic illustration of subordinates' tendencies to give a detailed background briefing to their readers.

TO: Division President

FROM: Sarah Smith

SUBJECT: Energy Conservation

Last year we set a goal to reduce energy usage by 7 percent. We have met that goal; actual energy expenditures amount to only 93 percent of last year's.

Furthermore, since A & B Corporation grew by 6 percent this year, the energy reduction actually exceeded our goal—probably in the range of a 10 percent to 13 percent reduction. A survey of all operations indicated that additional reductions in energy usage will be difficult. And considering the almost unpredictable but sky-rocketing costs of energy, A & B faces a future energy conservation dilemma.

Energy usage will grow in Chicago because of increased computer utilization and additional automated production equipment. However, the solar project and the substitution of a small boiler for a large one in the cafeteria should increase energy conservation in Dallas. Also, in Palo Alto, several conservation projects, including weekend shutdown of air conditioning, will contribute to overall savings.

With this background in mind, would you please either convene a meeting yourself, or authorize me to convene one to discuss the impact of future energy conservation on A & B's operations? If you need any further information before making your decision, please let me know.

If you were the boss, would you think all this background briefing was really necessary? Possibly. But the writer's decision to put the background before the purpose doesn't give the reader a choice. That choice should be made by the reader, not the writer. According to bottom-line rule 3, the memo should begin like this:

TO: Division President

FROM: Sarah Smith

SUBJECT: Energy Conservation

I am pleased to report that A & B Corporation is doing very well in conserving energy. On the other hand, we face a future energy conservation dilemma. Therefore, I request that:

1. You convene a meeting yourself, or
2. Authorize me to convene a meeting to discuss the impact of future energy conservation on A & B Corporation's operations.

Here is the background you may need to keep in mind as you consider this matter:

1. _____
2. _____
3. _____

Ask yourself, if you were the top executive, which of these two approaches would you prefer? Do you enjoy searching for bottom lines? We strongly believe you'd prefer the bottom-line revision according to bottom-line rule 3.

5

THREE MORE RULES
TO KEEP YOU
FROM BACKSLIDING

At the beginning of section 4, we mentioned that there are four relapses you have to avoid in order to continue creating bottom-line messages. So far we have examined two. Here are the other two:

Relapse 3: Burying your action request so thoroughly that your readers have no idea what you want them to do.

Relapse 4: Presenting information in a helter-skelter pattern, rather than in the order of its importance to your reader.

Now look at three bottom-line rules that combat these relapses.

BOTTOM-LINE RULE 4: ALWAYS HIGH-IMPACT AN ACTION REQUEST—AND BOTTOM-LINE IT IF APPROPRIATE.

When writers seek to persuade a reader to take a requested action, they are invariably leery of coming right out with their request, especially when they are writing upward in their organization. In training sessions where both managers and non-managers are present, we see a clear difference between memos written downward by the managers and memos written upward by the subordinates. People writing down feel completely free to bottom-line their action requests. Frequently, their memos simply amount to no more than this:

TO: Subordinate

FROM: Superior

Please do the following:
1. _____
2. _____
3. _____

But when subordinates are writing up to their manager, they find themselves very reluctant to make their action request stand out clearly for the boss's attention. Not only do subordinates violate bottom-line rule 3 and go through a long song and dance about why they have had the audacity to ask something of the boss, but they also tend to bury their action requests so thoroughly that frequently the boss has no clear notion of what he or she is being asked to do.

Such feelings are very widespread. In our training sessions, we often single out some outspoken member of the management group and ask why he or she bottom-lines action requests. Invariably the answer goes like this:

> Because I am a risk-taker. I am not afraid to give orders. When I know something needs to be done, I order it done.

However, we soon put this brave statement to the test by assigning a case where the managers are now the subordinates of a higher-level manager. Now they have to make a request upward. Immediately, these managers, including the supposedly outspoken and brave ones, reverse form, beat around the bush, and finally (in obscure, unemphasized terms) bury their requests in the middle of a fat third or fourth paragraph.

Here is a typical instance of this phenomenon at work. J. B. Cowden is a lower-level staff assistant in corporate headquarters who was asked to ensure that the various plant locations conserve gasoline. She wrote the following letter to three high-level executives who are plant managers at each of these locations. These managers far outranked Cowden. Consequently, she wrote the following letter.

Memo F

TO: Ms. R. B. Dickham
             Mr. S. V. Madden
             Ms. R. A. Wiegand

FROM: Jane B. Cowden

SUBJECT: Gasoline Shortage Contingency Planning

Recently I asked each of you to update your location fuel shortage contingency plan for car pooling, shuttle buses, and so on. Now gasoline supplies vary from location to location, and we believe that shortages will continue.

L. G. Lees, A & B Program Manager of Safety, has been designated as the division focal point for this problem. His mission is to coordinate A & B programs relating to gasoline shortages as they affect:

1. Employee ability to get to and from work.
2. Requirements for local mileage at major locations.
3. Occasional and regular driver programs.

Please designate an individual at your location to work with Mr. Lees in this effort. He can be reached on Extension 2222; advise him of your designee as soon as possible.

A. R. Gregg retains his responsibility as the Division Energy Coordinator for facilities.

Finally, it is in A & B's best interest that we continue to provide our employees with assistance in locating others interested in car pooling. Therefore, you should periodically remind employees of the availability of this service.

Put yourself in the reader's place. Just what are you being asked to do? As a plant manager, you are busy. You have important things to do. You can't waste time trying to figure out just what the writer wants you to do. Her letter goes back to the pile on your desk to wait until you have more time to figure it out. Two weeks later it's still sitting there.

Wouldn't it have been far better if she had written to these top executives in the fashion of bottom-lined memo F? And why shouldn't she? Is there any real threat to her by bottom-lining the actions she requests at the beginning of the memo? We don't think so.

Memo F—Bottom-Lined

TO: Ms. R. B. Dickham
            Mr. S. V. Madden
            Ms. R. A. Wiegand

FROM: Jane B. Cowden

SUBJECT: Gasoline Shortage Contingency Planning

So that your updated fuel shortage contingency plan can be implemented effectively, please:
1. Designate an individual at your location to work with L. G. Lees, A & B Program Manager of Safety, who has been named as the divisional focal point for this problem.
2. Periodically remind employees that we will continue to provide them with assistance in locating others interested in car pooling.

Even if in your best judgment the action request should not be placed at the very beginning of the letter, it still should be expressed in a high-impact fashion: indented, listed, surrounded by white space, virtually leaping off the page to the reader's attention. The more you can make action requests look like checklists, the better chance you have of getting your reader to do what you want.

A psychologist at Harvard University was asked once, "What's the best way of getting people to do what you want?" His answer was, "Ask them!" So, if the best way of getting people to do what you want is to ask them, and if there are numerous actions being requested, then make it simple for readers to check off each of the requests as they are complied with.

BOTTOM-LINE RULE 5: BOTTOM-LINE INFORMATION IN ORDER OF ITS IMPORTANCE TO THE READER.

Don't organize information for presentation to your reader based on your own interests. Organize it in terms of each item's importance to the reader. We are going through an information explosion that requires all sensible readers to be guarded about what they are going to spend time reading. Just ask yourself how you approach reading a lengthy document that is intended to convey information to you. Don't you ask yourself:

A. What kind of information does this report contain? And is this information:

1. Important to me?
2. Of probable use to me?
3. Of possible use to me?
4. Of no relevance to my interest?

If you as a reader find that the answer to question 1 is yes, you will go on and read the details. If the answer to question 2 is yes, you will read somewhat suspiciously, ready to stop if the probable utility of the information decreases.

If the answer to question 3 is yes, you will probably quickly scan the document to see if the information is, in fact, of any possible use.

If the information is of no use or relevance to you, it belongs in the wastebasket.

As a writer, you must make decisions based on how you think the reader will respond to questions 1 through 4. But the problem you may face is this: often you simply have no idea what the reader will think is important. What can you do?

The next bottom-line rule gives you the answer.

> BOTTOM-LINE RULE 6: PUT INFORMATION OF DUBIOUS UTILITY OR QUESTIONABLE IMPORTANCE TO THE READER INTO AN APPENDIX. (THIS ALSO APPLIES TO DETAILED INFORMATION THAT PROBABLY WILL NOT BE READ IN ITS ENTIRETY BY THE RECIPIENT.)

Let's see how bottom-line rules 5 and 6 can be applied to the following memo, which informs branch personnel managers about a corporate founder's college scholarship award.

TO: Branch Personnel Managers

FROM: Headquarters Personnel

SUBJECT: Scholarship Qualifying Test

The Preliminary Scholarship Aptitude Test/National Merit Scholarship Qualifying Test (PSAT/NMSQT) will be given at selected overseas high schools on either October 23 or 27 (as determined by the individual schools).

Brochures describing the details of the program will be distributed by this office in August.

Students who are entering their junior year at an overseas location this fall should check now with their principals to see if the test will be administered at their school so they can register for it. If their school does not plan to give the test, the student or principal should write to PSAT/NMSQT, Box 589, Princeton, New Jersey 08540, before July 6, to determine alternative testing locations.

If your location has employees on overseas assignments, you should pass this information along to them, since the PSAT/NMSQT is used as the basis for selecting A & B founders' award college scholarships.

Suppose some—or most—of the branches of A & B do not have employees on overseas assignments. Why should the writer force all branch personnel managers to wade through information that is of no relevance whatsoever to them?

Let's look at this same memo organized according to bottom-line rules 5 and 6:

TO: Branch Personnel Managers

FROM: Headquarters Personnel

SUBJECT: Scholarship Qualifying Test

If your location has—or will have—employees on overseas assignment who have high-school-age children, the attached information is important. It contains details of how these employees' children may compete while overseas for an A & B founders' award college scholarship.

Notice how much more considerate the revision is. If the branch personnel managers don't have employees with high-school-age children overseas, they know immediately that they need read no further.

6

LEAD YOUR READER BY THE NOSE THROUGH COMPLEX COMMUNICATIONS

Let's discuss how to bottom-line long, difficult, or complicated analytical reports.

A long report should make its organizational pattern clear at the beginning. Each subsection should state its purpose and proclaim how that subsection will be organized. This approach means that you tell readers where the report is going instead of allowing readers to infer the report's direction. Otherwise, all the ills of failing to bottom-line a short message will be many times multiplied because of the difficulty readers have in grasping the complexities of a long analytical report.

In long, complex documents there may be many bottom-line statements. In fact, in a multisection report, each subsection should have its own bottom line.

It is your responsibility as a writer to know how the various elements of your discussion fit together into a logical skeletal framework; it is also, above all, your responsibility to make that skeletal framework crystal clear to your reader. You must make it leap from the page to the reader's eye. The way you do that is through adherence to the following bottom-line rule.

> BOTTOM-LINE RULE 7: NEVER KEEP SECRET FROM THE READER (OR YOURSELF) THE DIRECTION(S) IN WHICH A COMPLICATED ANALYTICAL DISCUSSION WILL GO. MAKE A CONTRACT WITH YOUR READERS AND FULFILL EVERY CLAUSE OF THAT CONTRACT IN THE SAME SEQUENTIAL ORDER AS CONTRACTED.

A contract sentence is a guiding sentence that organizes, for both the reader and the writer, the direction of the remainder of the message. Contract sentences are primarily required in longer, complex documents. They usually follow immediately after the bottom-line sentence. And in long documents they should also occur at the beginning of subsections.

Here is an example of a bottom-line sentence followed by a contract sentence:

> This proposal recommends that you transfer to the XYZ Mobilized Transfer System (MTS). MTS was developed to answer the needs of growing systems like yours. Let me explain in more detail the reasons for this change—first in terms of the needs of your present environment, then in terms of MTS's adaptability to that environment.

Clearly, the reader expects the discussion to deal first with the needs of the company's environment for MTS, and second MTS's adaptability to that environment. That's the contract that has been made.

Here is another good example:

> There are three reasons why XYZ, Inc., should not be given our business:
> 1. Cost,
> 2. Quality,
> 3. Service.
> Let me elaborate on each point.

What should follow? A discussion of cost, quality, and service, obviously. Wouldn't all writers follow this sequence that they have contracted for? Surprisingly, no! Many writers will discuss service first, probably because service was the last item mentioned.

Then they might discuss either cost or quality. And they might completely forget to discuss either one of these factors. By forcing ourselves to adhere to the sequence of factors announced in the contract sentence, we force ourselves to be logical and coherent, rather than to allow our thoughts to jump all over the place. That is why we say that a good contract sentence organizes a document not only for the reader but for the writer as well.

Compare the following two shortened versions of a long report.

Version A

TO: J. Pounds

FROM: M. Watts

SUBJECT: Funding Allocations

I should like at this time to request that corporate headquarters make an allocation to the Biloxi division in order that Biloxi may be able to handle local situations which, for the most part, are of an emergency nature.

All of the department's financial business is handled at our division office; we are allocated no funds for local situations in Biloxi. In order to respond to problems at the Biloxi facility, we need some local funds to _____

_____

_____.

Internal Maintenance presently needs additional funds because of the recent flood. The flood shorted out our power station, and we are presently operating on temporary load borrowed from the city. Furthermore,....

Version B

TO: J. Pounds

FROM: M. Watts

SUBJECT: Funding Allocations

I am writing to request that corporate headquarters make an allocation to the Biloxi division in order that we may be able to handle local situations which, for the most part, are of an emergency nature. Let me first give you the background of our financial setup and, second, explain in some detail our present needs for additional funds.

Financial Setup. All of our department's financial business is handled at our division office; we are allocated no funds for local situations in Biloxi. In order to respond to problems at the Biloxi facility, we need some local funds to _____

_____.

Additional Funds Needs. Internal Maintenance presently needs additional funds because of the recent flood. The flood shorted out our power station, and we are presently operating on a temporary load borrowed from the city. Furthermore,....

Both versions begin with a bottom-line sentence. But note in version B how the contract sentence that immediately follows specifies what will be discussed. And the underlined subheadings clarify and make obvious the skeletal framework to the busy reader.

Now let's deal with an even more complicated report. Obviously, it would be dysfunctional for us to reproduce the complete text of a long analytical report in this book. Therefore, we'll just focus on the skeletal organization of such a report, and we'll see how to clarify the interaction of the main ideas of the report.

The report begins as follows:

I have divided my analysis of XYZ's plant problems into two separate parts. In the first part, I investigate what I feel to be the short-run problems in the plant: personnel turnover and transportation problems. Recommended solutions to these problems are also given.

In the second section, I investigate and recommend an approach to the less immediate problems of long-run growth: expansion and new products. In this section, I have implicitly accepted the idea that we should first concentrate on solving our immediate problems and, later, with an improved operating position, worry about the longer term.

The writer has organized the report for both the reader and himself or herself. The skeletal framework (which will become the headings and subheadings of the report) is as follows:

Part I: Short-Run Problems in Plant
   A. Personnel turnover
   B. Transportation problems
   C. Recommended solutions

Part II: Less Immediate Problems of Long-Run Growth
   A. Expansion
   B. New products

But, remember, we are dealing with a synopsis of a very long and complicated report. If this contract statement appears on page 1, what help will it be to readers when they get, say, to page 10? We recommend the following:

BOTTOM-LINE RULE 8: IN COMPLEX, MULTISECTIONED REPORTS, WRITE CONTRACT SENTENCES FOR EACH SUBSECTION THAT:

1. BOTTOM-LINE WHAT THAT SUBSECTION IS ABOUT.

2. MAKE A TRANSITION FROM PREVIOUS SUBSECTIONS TO THE PRESENT SUBSECTION (IF NEEDED).

3. SPECIFY CLEARLY THE TOPICS TO BE DISCUSSED IN THAT SUBSECTION.

If a report is extremely complicated, not only should each of its subsections (IA, IB, IC, IIA, and IIB) have a bottom-line statement summarizing the information given in that subsection, but each subsection also should present a new contract sentence. Let's take, as an example, subsection IIB.

IIB: Transportation Problems

Our study concludes that unless the difficulties our employees face in commuting to our satellite plant locations can be sharply alleviated, the unsatisfactory personnel turnover rate just described will, if anything, accelerate. The basic aspects of the transportation problem discussed in this section are as follows:

1. Traffic problems associated with an 8–5 work schedule.
2. Ever-escalating costs of gasoline and reliable automobiles.

3. Unlikely prospects of future mass transportation being funded in plant areas.
4. Lack of success with employee carpooling.

Writers sometimes argue about whether such transitional contract sentences seem labored and cumbersome to the reader. The answer is no. Never force your reader to infer your organizational pattern. Make it obvious. In fact, we urge you, in effect, to lead your reader by the nose through the labyrinth of your analysis.

But that applies only to long, complicated reports. And it applies only to communications that are not sensitive.

WHEN AND WHEN NOT
TO BOTTOM-LINE
SENSITIVE MESSAGES

7

CONSIDER RELATIONSHIP, POSITION, AND THE MESSAGE

Certain types of sensitive situations lead any sensible writer to think twice before bottom-lining. For instance, suppose you are trying to persuade a prominent businessperson to come and speak to your Rotary group. Should you begin directly with your request? Or should you first give some background information that stresses the benefits he or she might possibly receive by visiting your group?

Obviously, no magic formula exists that tells you when and when not to use a bottom-line approach in what we are defining as sensitive situations, that is, ones that cause or require emotional reactions in readers. A number of factors color the decision about whether or not to do so, including the type of relationship (close or distant) between the reader and the writer, the relative power positions of writer and reader, and the type of message being conveyed.

Naturally, if writers enjoy a close, mutually trusting relationship with their readers, they can probably use whatever organizational pattern they want. In fact, in such cases, as we will see, any appearance of trying to "con" the reader will be likely to prove detrimental not only to the success of the communication, but to the writer–reader relationship as well.

Also, whether you are writing up to someone in a higher power position, or down to a subordinate or someone dependent on your good will, makes a decided difference in the decision of whether to bottom-line.

Fortunately, since all sensitive message situations arise from one of three types of messages—positive, negative, or persuasive—we can offer some general advice about bottom-lining that takes into account the type of message being sent and whether it is being sent up or down.

We leave it up to you to factor into your decision whether or not you are close to the reader.

Our general advice about how to organize various types of messages will be discussed in detail in 8 and 9. We will show that there are actually only two basic types of organizational patterns: the direct (or bottom-lined) approach and the circuitous approach.

1. *The direct pattern* is for information that can and should be bottom-lined, that is, presented as quickly and straightforwardly as possible. This approach, therefore, would be used in:
   - Information-conveying messages—up or down.
   - Positive messages—up or down.
   - Positive/persuasive messages—up or down.
   - Negative messages—down.

2. *The circuitous pattern* is for information that should not be forthrightly and promptly disclosed but should be held back until the reader's mind has been conditioned and prepared for that information. This pattern, therefore, would be used in:
   - Negative messages—up.
   - Negative/persuasive messages—up or down.
   - Blind/persuasive messages—up or down.
   - Any type of messages where the writer has sensible reasons to fear being forthright—up.

Which of these patterns is preferable for you to use depends on the type of message being written.

8

FOUR SENSITIVE MESSAGES YOU CAN BOTTOM-LINE EFFICIENTLY

BOTTOM-LINE POSITIVE MESSAGES

There are no valid reasons for not bottom-lining a positive communication. Why be circuitous when writing good news such as "You got the raise"? Nevertheless, businesspeople have such resistance to bottom-lining any message that they will all too frequently organize good-news letters according to the same circuitous pattern they tend to use for *all* messages. Because of managers' innate tendency to bury their purpose, they often end up writing good-news memos that actually read like bad news. Check your own correspondence to see whether you have this tendency. Adherence to bottom-line rule 9 solves the problem.

> BOTTOM-LINE RULE 9: ALWAYS BOTTOM-LINE THE GOOD NEWS; THERE IS NO CONFLICT BETWEEN BOT-TOM-LINING AND POSITIVE MESSAGES.

Below is a real-life memo that shows how foolish it is not to use a direct approach with good news. Employees at a headquarters location received this memo by desktop distribution. Because of building construction at that location, parking had already become a troublesome problem. If you were one of these already irritated employees, how would this memo have struck you?

TO: All Employees at Pebble Brook Location

FROM: R. T. Thomas

As you know, construction of the new building at Pebble Brook temporarily eliminated a number of parking spaces. In order for the Gulf Coast Assurance Company to begin construction of its fifth building, the parking presently utilized in this area will be eliminated on Wednesday, May 2.

Gulf Coast has converted several of the landscaped areas around the parking lots to temporary parking until parking under construction is completed. These temporary areas provide 43 spaces as a net addition to those lost to construction of both new buildings.

The first phase of 100 spaces in the new parking area is scheduled for partial completion by October 1, with total completion by December 1.

The first paragraph undoubtedly will infuriate the reader: "What? You mean we are going to have even *fewer* parking spaces than we have now?" And there is the danger that the reader, in irritation, will slam the memo into the wastebasket. The fact that the message actually conveys good news is completely masked by the circuitous organizational pattern that buries the good news at the end of the second paragraph.

Clearly, in an essentially positive situation like this, bottom-lining will significantly improve the emotional reaction of your reader. A bottom-lined message like the following would obviously have done a much better job:

TO: All Employees at Pebble Brook Location

FROM: R. T. Thomas

You will be pleased to learn that soon we will have 43 additional parking spaces. These result from a conversion of several landscaped areas into a temporary parking lot....

POSITIVE PERSUASIVE REQUESTS

BOTTOM-LINE RULE 10: IN POSITIVE PERSUASIVE SITUA-
TIONS, WHERE YOU DO NOT
KNOW HOW YOUR READER
WILL REACT TO WHAT YOU ASK
FOR, BOTTOM-LINE YOUR RE-
QUEST IN ALL CASES EXCEPT:

1. THOSE IN WHICH YOU DON'T
(OR BARELY) KNOW THE
READER, AND TO ASK SOME-
THING IMMEDIATELY OF A
RELATIVE (OR ABSOLUTE)
STRANGER WOULD PROBA-
BLY BE PERCEIVED AS
"PUSHY."

2. THOSE IN WHICH THE RELA-
TIONSHIP BETWEEN YOU
AND YOUR READER IS NOT
CLOSE OR WARM.

There is a big difference between how you organize a positive persuasive message and how you organize a negative persuasive one. For now, let's just examine positive persuasive messages. In a positive persuasive message, the writer is trying to persuade readers to do something that is obviously for their own good, such as:

- "Be sure to register your vacation plans with my office before April 25, so that we have plenty of time to iron out any conflicts that arise."
- "Doctors predict serious flu outbreaks this coming winter. Be sure to get your flu shot at the infirmary right away!"

When your task is to persuade readers to do something for their own good—and it is obvious to those readers that what you ask is for their own good—then bottom-line the message and use a direct organizational pattern.

It doesn't matter much whether you are writing up or down. If you are trying to persuade your boss (or your best customer) to do what is good for him or her, what's wrong with bottom-lining your suggestion?

Yet, if you check your files, you quite possibly will see that, like most writers, you don't bottom-line much of anything, regardless of the type of message you are sending. Look at what happened in the following memo:

MEMORANDUM TO: XYZ Employees

SUBJECT: Shuttle-Bus Service

As you are aware, we are having a number of traffic problems between our Pebble Brook and Valleyview buildings. Employees are taking their vehicles from one building to the other and are parking in slots not assigned to them. Naturally, when an employee's slot is taken, he or she parks elsewhere—usually in another person's slot—and complicates matters further. The end result of all this is hurt feelings and damaged employee morale.

To combat this problem, a parking and traffic committee was formed to suggest solutions. After studying a number of alternatives, the committee recommended a shuttle-bus service between the buildings. We urge you to use this service.

In ninety days it will be monitored and evaluated for usage, energy savings, and other benefits; the service will be continued or terminated based on this evaluation.

Details of the service are....

You cannot fail to notice that the writer has used a circuitous organizational pattern better suited to a negative message. It beats around the bush and doesn't get to its purpose until the middle of the second paragraph, where the committee's recommendation of a shuttle service has been carefully buried.

But what's so negative about this shuttle service? Won't it solve or at least alleviate a problem that has been bothering all personnel? Isn't this message really positive persuasive? If so, it should have been bottom-lined like this:

MEMORANDUM TO: XYZ Employees

SUBJECT: Shuttle-Bus Service

We are pleased to announce a new shuttle-bus service between our Pebble Brook and Valleyview buildings. This service will begin on June 4 and will allow you to go from building to building without using your own vehicles.

BLIND PERSUASIVE SITUATIONS

Blind persuasive messages are sent to readers we know little or nothing about, except that their names may have appeared on a mailing list of people supposed to have certain characteristics in common. Much of the direct mail we receive falls into this category. Writers of this type of message don't know for certain whether what they are selling or asking will be perceived as positive or negative by their readers. Consequently, most direct mail pieces are circuitously organized—what is being asked or sold is not sprung upon the reader until the writer has had a chance to condition the reader's mind to be receptive to the request.

For the same reason, many young businesspeople, fresh from a course on effective selling, often resist bottom-line techniques. Their instructors have convinced them that winning over a potential customer requires an organizational pattern (oral or written), beginning with a pitch that will 1) rivet the customer's attention on the product, and 2) dramatize all of the wondrous benefits this fine product will bring to the customer. Only after accomplishing these necessary preliminaries can salespeople dare to admit to the customer (or reader) that their purpose is to sell something.

Personally, we regard it as debatable whether any customers are actually fooled by a salesperson's song and dance. Most customers, we suspect, observe the goings-on with general amusement and regard them as a sort of ritual that must be suffered through.

But we do not wish to get into a debate with successful marketers on this point. Certainly, an exception to bottom-lining may be justified when you are making a cold call on a potential customer. But most persuasive writing situations are not cold calls. (Admittedly, direct-mail letters are cold calls, even though market research and specialized mailing lists can tell the writer much about the reader's age, sex, religion, politics, education, hobbies, work, and the like.) But with the possible exception of direct mail, when do you write completely blindly?

For example, when you write a cover letter to a lengthy, detailed sales proposal, it will indeed 1) be short and bottom-lined, and 2) ask for that order. It would be foolish to pretend that the readers don't know they are being asked to buy something!

The sales proposal itself might not be bottom-lined. It might follow a format very similar to that followed by scientific papers:

1. A definition of the problem to be analyzed (e.g., a statement of the customer's needs).
2. A statement of how the seller's product will solve the customer's problems.
3. A detailed analysis of benefits and/or savings produced by the seller's product.
4. A statement of what the product will cost.
5. A request for the order (the bottom line at last!).

But the covering letter will not be organized in the same circuitous (if "scientific") fashion. It will be organized in the same way as a personal interview with a potential customer. There the customer sits, fidgeting and looking at his watch. You know he is extremely busy, so you are not going to go through the long, formal, scientific organizational pattern used by the sales proposal. The customer literally wouldn't sit still for it.

The customer knows perfectly well that you have been analyzing his operation, so you won't risk being coy and beating around the bush before getting to the point. You will organize the presentation according to how you believe the busy customer's mind expects information to be presented:

1. Here's the problem causing trouble.
2. Here's the solution we can offer.
3. Here's our proof that our solution will work.
4. May we have your business?

In fact, no significant conflict exists between bottom-lining and the principles of effective selling—except, perhaps, when you are making a cold call on people who might throw you out of the office if you admitted you were selling a product that, at first glance, they probably won't like.

But what about bottom-lining in internal persuasive situations that are blind only because writers have no idea about whether readers will perceive what they ask as positive or negative in

respect to their interests? If, for example, you are
persuade your boss to increase your department...
should you come right out and bottom-line your purpose? Or
should you treat the boss as if he or she were a cold call and try to
get the boss's attention, show the benefits of increasing your
departmental budget, and then get around to asking for what
you want? Good question!

Naturally, in a real-life situation, you have to make this type of
judgment. But if you have even a reasonably close working
relationship with your boss, a direct-mail approach that attempts
to con the boss runs a real risk of boomeranging. First of all,
you'll fool nobody. Certainly, by the time the boss has finished
reading the memo, he or she knows full well what is being asked.
So why not bottom-line the request in the first place? Why use
the fact that you are writing a persuasive message to justify
beating around the bush, wasting your boss's time, and probably
looking far less businesslike than you would if you came out
directly with the request?

NEGATIVE MESSAGE DOWNWARD

If you are writing downward, you *are* the boss and can probably
write any way you like. But while you don't want to be overbearing, you want to avoid sounding wishy-washy. Besides, subordinates expect you to give orders and approach tasks directly and
forcefully. The majority of businesspeople we have worked with
regard it as sheer artifice for a superior to beat around the bush
and not bottom-line bad news sent to subordinates. Bottom-line
rule 11, therefore, states:

> BOTTOM-LINE RULE 11: BOTTOM-LINE DOWNWARD
> NEGATIVE MESSAGES UN-
> LESS EXTENUATING CIRCUM-
> STANCES ARE INVOLVED.

We do suggest, however, that you consider the following bits
of advice if you choose to employ a bottom-line pattern in a
negative situation:

- Stress to the reader that you are being straightforward and
  honest (you are, so you might as well receive credit for it).

For example, you might begin, "Jim, I'm going to be honest with you about the Simmons account. I know that you have put a terrific effort into bringing the account into line with our expectations. But despite all your work, outside factors have kept you from achieving the goal."

- Stress or imply that you are being straightforward because:
    1. You know the reader appreciates directness.
    2. You would never run the risk of seeming to con someone you respect as much as you do your reader.

For instance, you might say, "Sarah, you and I have always enjoyed a straightforward relationship. So let me tell you right off that I think these are three reasons why your plans won't work."

- Temper your direct approach with kudos for the reader.

"If anyone could have salvaged this project from the wastebasket, it was you. In fact, the project only survived as long as it did thanks to your untiring devotion."

- Whenever possible, include explanations for a negative decision along with the decision.

Few people will take no for an answer and not ask for an explanation. That is the problem with bottom-line letters that state:

Dear Subordinate:

The answer to your question is no.

But the fault is not in the direct organizational pattern used; it lies in the lack of explanation. Even your children ask "Why?" when you tell them no. Negative situations, therefore, require conscious adaptation to the reader, both in terms of the message presented and the style of writing.

The following negative letter is bottom-lined. Yet the direct organizational pattern probably would be more acceptable to the reader than would an indirect approach that might sound artificial and insincere.

TO: Subordinate

FROM: Boss

You have worked so hard on the XYZ campaign that I owe it to you not to keep you in suspense. I cannot recommend that your program be implemented.

Because you know of my respect for your creative abilities, I know you will want me to be forthright about the reasons behind this decision.

   1. _____

   2. _____

   3. _____

9

TWO SENSITIVE MESSAGES YOU SHOULD THINK TWICE ABOUT BEFORE BOTTOM-LINING

So far we have discussed sensitive situations where bottom-lining applies. Now let's take up the two situations—both negative—where a circuitous, non-bottom-lined approach will probably be better. Such situations involve:

1. Negative messages—up.
2. Negative persuasive messages—up or down.

NEGATIVE MESSAGES UPWARD

One of the oddities of business writing practice is the fact that many people who refuse to bottom-line a message as inconsequential and nonsensitive as "Let's encourage car pooling among our employees" will bottom-line a highly sensitive negative message. Perhaps this is because they simply get so nervous about their writing task that they literally blurt out, "Dear Sir, No!"

And the one sure time to think twice before bottom-lining is when you are writing a negative message upward.

One of the most difficult situations any writer faces is writing to a superior—a boss or a powerful customer—to convey bad news. This kind of letter, though written infrequently, is extremely delicate. Bottom-lining such a letter can be suicidal. For example:

TO: Boss

FROM: Subordinate

There are three reasons why your plan won't work:
1. It costs too much.
2. The quality of the product cannot be controlled.
3. It is impossible to offer adequate field service.

Bottom-lined? You bet! Smart? Probably not, unless the writer and the boss have a marvelous relationship. That is why we have developed this rule:

BOTTOM-LINE RULE 12: THINK TWICE BEFORE BOTTOM-LINING NEGATIVE MESSAGES UPWARD.

If, in your professional judgment, a bottom-line approach in a negative letter to someone in a higher power position might hammer its point home too bluntly (or seemingly curtly), then you are wise to select a different organizational tool from your writing workbench—one that is more useful in this delicate task. That tool, the circuitous organizational pattern, basically requires that you take four steps in writing negative messages:

1. A pleasant, cordial—or at least neutral—beginning.
2. An explanation of the reasons for the negative message.
3. A statement of the negative message in flat, low-impact terms.
4. A pleasant, get-off-the-subject ending.

Let's apply this advice to the above memo and see what it might look like.

TO: Boss

FROM: Subordinate

At your request a careful analysis of your plan has been conducted. This analysis has revealed many good points about the plan. Specifically, it will:

1. _____
2. _____
3. _____

But, while the plan will accomplish much, some might feel that further consideration should be given to some factors that might conceivably produce less than hoped for consequences. We mention these only for the purpose of enabling you to add possible refinements to an already valuable plan of action.

Here are the areas on which, we feel sure, you will want to bring to bear your analytical skills and practical experience:

1. Cost....
2. Quality....
3. Service....

Of course, there's an obvious danger to using a circuitous organizational pattern. While some (probably most) readers will perceive your pattern as polite, sensitive, and courteous, others will think that you are trying to con them and may resent it.

For this reason we say, "Think twice before bottom-lining negative messages upward." We cannot tell you to do one or the other. But whatever you do, do it by design, not by accident.

Are there ways to avoid appearing transparent in negative situations? We think so. We think it is possible to be tactful, sensitive, and courteous, and still be honest.

Suppose a very large customer writes and describes a problem with XYZ drive shafts. The reader has the problem studied and learns that his company is in no way responsible for the problem. Therefore, he dictates the following bottom-lined explanation to the customer who is, obviously, in a position equivalent to that of a superior.

Ms. Mary Smith
Smith Industries
455 North Cane Street
Atlanta, GA 30303

Dear Ms. Smith:

We are not responsible for the cracking problems you encountered with our drive shafts. The fault lies with the way the casing is installed. Our contract states installation is your responsibility.

We appreciate your business and look forward to future dealings with you. Let us know if we can help you in any way.

Let's assume that you are a consultant to the writer. At his request, you examine this letter carefully when it gets back from typing. Something is wrong. For one thing, it's too blunt. Some kind of padding is needed. Also, the letter doesn't give the writer due credit for all the work he did. After all, he did a lot of research to come up with this bottom-line answer. After some consideration, you recommend that the writer try a circuitous organizational pattern in a second draft:

Dear Ms. Smith:

Thank you for your letter reporting the cracking problems you have encountered with our drive shafts.

Since many of the industries we supply have experienced similar problems, we have done a great deal of research into this situation. Our studies show that the fault usually lies with the way a customer or some outside contractor has installed the casing.

I hope this answer leads to a solution for you. Let me know if I can help in any other way.

The circuitous pattern obviously dulls some of the impact. But isn't the technique obvious? In essence, the letter says:

1. Thanks for writing.
2. The problem is not ours.
3. Good luck in solving it.

The letter may not be organized in a bottom-line fashion, but the message is. And that message is clear: It's your problem, not ours!

If Ms. Smith is a good customer and if you want to retain her good will—and her account—but you do not want to accept responsibility for the problem, then you had better get to work on this letter and try to develop a third, more effective revision:

Dear Ms. Smith:

Thank you for your letter expressing concern about the drive shaft casings we supplied. Since everyone at XYZ, Inc., appreciates the significant amount of business you do with us, I immediately began a search to see if we could find some ways of resolving the problem for you.

What I have done for you.

After receiving your letter, I first met with John Davis, Head of Product Design, and members of our structural engineering staff. We reexamined all of the design components and checked to make sure that the drive shaft we supplied met your requested specifications. Since it did, we decided to look elsewhere for the cracking problem.

Problems other companies had.

About two years ago ABC, Inc. experienced a similar problem with a casing we had provided. I therefore called Mary Church at ABC and asked if ABC's engineers had resolved the problem. Mary told me that after an extensive analysis, ABC's design engineers found that the cause of the problem was the installation procedure used at ABC. ABC utilized a torque molding approach when installing the drive shaft. This approach applied too much tension to the casing and caused some hairline cracks within it. Eventually, these cracks widened and the problem you described resulted.

Personalized solution.

ABC resolved the problem by shifting to a drive centimeter system and has had no problem since this change. I know that you use a drive torque approach. You may therefore want to give some consideration to the possibility that it is causing some of the problem.

I also checked with some structural engineering consultants at Carnegie-Mellon. The consultants said that they had heard of problems similar to yours in a variety of

For you, I went beyond the realm of normal assistance.

industries that use casings with the dimensions you requested. They said that many of these problems were solved by rechecking the design and by shortening the steel mold used on the front end. Apparently, the mold sometimes catches onto the train shaft, applying pressure. This pressure eventually causes cracks.

Here's what to do.

The mold also seems to allow some moisture into the casing, which of course also results in gradual damage. I am sure you will want to have your engineers look into this as a possible reason for the cracking.

We'll help all we can.

Ms. Smith, if this latter situation proves to be a cause of the problem, we will be more than happy to work with you on redesigning the casing dimensions.

You are pleased with this draft and especially note how the writer:

1. Shifts between being personal when talking about what the writer did for the reader, and being impersonal when talking specifically about Smith Industries' problems.
2. Creates distance between the writer's own company, XYZ, and the design problems. The major problems are revealed by Mary Church at ABC and by engineering consultants at Carnegie-Mellon.
3. Offers conclusions in a circuitous, diplomatic fashion. The suggested corrections come after, not before, the analysis and are not lumped together in a high-impact, punchy fashion. Obviously, the writer thought that a high-impact approach, though clear, might prove dangerous.
4. Goes into extreme detail about everything. The basic sentence structure is high-impact and straightforward, but the very length of the passage invites a "Thank you for the answer; I'll have engineering examine it" response.

But why are we extolling a non-bottom-lined letter? Because, above all, bottom-lining means writing in a way that gets a job done with the least amount of words, time, and effort being extended.

Obviously, the third version is longer and took more time to write. But if the first two versions had seriously offended Ms. Smith, how much additional correspondence and/or crow-eating visits might have been required? And how much time and energy would these have consumed?

NEGATIVE PERSUASIVE MESSAGES

> BOTTOM-LINE RULE 13: USE A CIRCUITOUS ORGANIZA-
> TIONAL PATTERN IN NEGATIVE
> REQUESTS WRITTEN TO PER-
> SONS IN HIGHER POWER POSI-
> TIONS, BUT STILL HIGH-IMPACT
> YOUR ACTION REQUEST.

In a negative persuasive message, the writer has the task of persuading readers to do something they do not want to do. The writer knows that the reader will perceive nothing good whatsoever about the request. For example:

> The Community Fund has asked A&BC to make an extra effort this year. Therefore, we are asking all employees to double their last year's contribution.

> Because of our new policy calling for reductions in manpower at our New Orleans site, we are offering you an assignment with our R&D group in Fargo, North Dakota.

Wise writers approach negative persuasive situations much more gingerly than positive persuasive situations where readers think the writer is trying to get them to do something for their own good.

What about messages where you have to persuade people to do something they don't want to do? A lot depends on whether your reader is a superior or not.

If you are routing a negative persuasive message down to a subordinate or to a supplier dependent on your good will, you can organize your message any way you like. But because this type of situation calls for even a boss to be persuasive (and not be able simply to give an order), a circuitous pattern is probably necessary. We doubt that bottom-lining would be effective in a letter where a boss asks you to double your Community Fund pledge.

And when you are trying to persuade a reader superior to you—your boss or your best customer—to do something he or she doesn't want to do, that request should not be bottom-lined.

Bottom-lining negative requests provides readers with an opportunity to counter your arguments. Once readers know you are trying to get them to do something they really don't want to do, they have an opportunity to dredge up contradictory arguments, remember opposite viewpoints, and generally oppose whatever you have said. This is not the kind of freedom you want to give readers when you are trying to convince them to do something they don't want to do.

Suppose, for example, you receive the following bottom-lined memo from your boss:

Dear Subordinate:

Next year's budget for your department has been reduced by $50K, from $555K to $505K.

I'm sure you know other areas are experiencing similar or even more drastic cuts. All of these cuts are because of the unexpected downturn in economic activity.

Suppose further that you believe your department simply cannot swallow such a drastic cut. You believe you have evidence to support your position. Would a bottom-line response be appropriate? Not with most superiors.

Dear Boss:

I cannot accept your decimation of my budget.

A circuitous path would provide a much more acceptable (and safer) approach to the problem. This message would:

1. Diplomatically acknowledge that budget tightening is definitely needed.
2. Note that a surgeon's knife does a better job than a shotgun in most budget-cutting operations.
3. Examine the ramifications of this budget cutting on your department's ability to achieve its assigned goals.
4. Specifically, but respectfully, request reconsideration of the cuts applied to your department.

One aspect of the above outline needs repeating: Specifically request reconsideration of the cuts applied to your department. Too often writers become so enamored of the circuitous style that they embed or hide the request being made. There will be no chance of reconsideration if the request never is brought to the reader's attention. Be sure the reader finds and understands a request even in negative persuasive messages.

In the following situation, the boss was in favor of immediately implementing a voluntary education program for the corporation. A subordinate attempted to persuade the boss to delay implementation of the program:

TO: Boss

FROM: Subordinate

Bill Blaze has completed the study of a voluntary education program for headquarters staff. Bill reviewed his findings with me on January 14.

In summary, Bill found that the recent history of voluntary education programs at other sites indicates diminishing employee interest. Additionally, support expense increases both in terms of equipment costs and instructor–student ratio.

Local schools and colleges provide a wide variety of programs at minimal cost. Headquarters personnel can communicate related information about these external programs to management and employees.

This avenue means that although consideration of a formal program might need to be postponed, a reading is needed on employee interest and participation in such programs. Additionally, further investigation of self-study courses should provide helpful data for future alternatives.

Needless to say, it takes a great deal of effort and interpretation even to guess at the action being requested. The following approach would have been much more effective:

TO: Boss

FROM: Subordinate

Bill Blaze has completed the study of a voluntary education program for headquarters staff. Bill reviewed his findings with me on January 14.

In summary, Bill found that the recent history of in-house training at other sites indicates diminishing employee interest. Additionally, support expense increases both in terms of equipment costs and instructor–student ratio.

Local schools and colleges provide a wide variety of programs at minimal cost. Headquarters personnel can communicate related information about these external programs to management and employees.

Bill's findings lead me to recommend that we not implement such a program at this time. Instead, for now, we should:

1. Gather a reading on employee interest and participation in such programs.
2. Study the possibility of further using guided learning centers.

This revision is just as tactfully circuitous. But the writer has made it far more likely that the boss will give serious consideration to the actions suggested.

MASTERING
THE MIND-SET
OF BOTTOM-LINE
WRITING

10

USE THE "SO WHAT?" FACTOR TO RECOGNIZE BOTTOM-LINE SENTENCES

Part III, which includes sections 10 and 11, offers you an opportunity to study, develop, and refine your bottom-line abilities. It shows you: a) how to respond instinctively in a bottom-line fashion in every appropriate situation, and b) offers models and examples of various bottom-line techniques you need to master. A methodology for learning to write in a bottom-line manner is also presented.

Bottom-lining is the key to incisive thought, and it does not always come easy. Many of the following examples will make you think hard before you plunge right to the heart of a message.

But the payoff may be great. All successful men and women of action are noted for their ability to cut through the unessential to the critical and to make crystal clear what they want and why. These sections will help you become that type of person.

Ten teaches you to distinguish bottom-line from non-bottom-line sentences, a skill necessary for becoming a bottom-line writer. Eleven will show you how to write acceptable first drafts of memos and letters. Taken together—and studied carefully— they provide a nuts-and-bolts methodology through which you can become an effective bottom-line writer.

RECOGNIZING A BOTTOM-LINE SENTENCE

Bottom-line writers need to be able to recognize a bottom-line sentence. If you cannot recognize a bottom-line sentence, how can you ever hope to write one?

Not everyone can distinguish a bottom-line from a non-bottom-line sentence. When we began conducting bottom-line training classes, we were not surprised to find that managers had problems identifying the bottom line in memos written to them. We were surprised to discover that some managers can't point out bottom-line sentences in memos they themselves have written!

The most effective way to separate bottom-line from non-bottom-line sentences is to apply the "So what?" factor. When you read a memo or letter, especially its first two or three sentences, ask yourself, "So what? What does this have to do with me?"

Look at the following three sample beginnings and ask, "So what?" about each. Assume each example is the first sentence in an unsolicited memo or letter. Furthermore, assume you have *not* requested the information conveyed.

1. The proposals from Jewel Mineral Castings arrived Thursday.
2. Employees are being task-trained in five areas.
3. On January 13, 198–, Mary Gobel represented XYZ Headquarters at the Fire Safety Task Force.

Aren't you inclined to respond like this?

Non-Bottom-Line Beginning	*Likely Response*
1. The proposals from Jewel Mineral Castings arrived Thursday.	So what? Why are you telling me this?

2. Employees are being task-trained in five areas.

That's nice, but what's that to me?

3. On January 13, 198–, Mary Gobel represented XYZ Headquarters at the Fire Safety Task Force.

So what?

Doesn't each of these likely responses, by irritating the reader, actually undercut the significance of the message that follows?

Now look what happens when these beginnings are recast into bottom-line statements:

Non-Bottom-Line Beginning	Revised Bottom-Line Beginning	Reader Response to Revision
1. The proposals from Jewel Mineral Castings arrived Thursday.	Unless you have objections I plan to place an order on Tuesday for twelve XYZ castings units at $135 each.	Fine!
2. Employees are being task-trained in five areas.	If your employees haven't received task training on the equipment they are assigned to operate, this training should be completed as soon as possible.	Will do!
3. On January 13, 198–, Mary Gobel represented XYZ Headquarters at the Fire Safety Task Force.	I am pleased to report that XYZ is in full compliance with fire safety standards.	Excellent!

In each bottom-line beginning, readers can recognize the message's purpose and can read further if they desire additional information.

Let's see if the "So what?" question can help you distinguish bottom-line from non-bottom-line sentences. Read the following three sentences, again assuming all are at the beginning of unsolicited memos or letters. Can you identify the bottom-line sentence?

Set A

1. Program/Assistance is a program product for accessing technical information from 1234 Terminal.
2. Please evaluate this product and encourage all departments within your business units to install and use it.
3. System programmers have easy access to technical information.

Obviously, once you asked "So what?" sentence 2 stands out as the only sentence that answers the question. Sentences 1 and 3 offer what may or may not end up being useful information.

Try asking "So what?" to the next two sets of sentences. See if it helps you identify the bottom-line sentences in each set.

Set B

4. As you are probably aware, this office is required to make a yearly report on the results of our negotiations.
5. I need to know the number of parcels acquired per professional grade employee as well as the percentage of tracts condemned. This information will enable me to ....
6. We realize that you have had no right-of-way work assigned other than nominal value signs.

Set C

7. The financial coordinator is responsible for five separate activities.
8. The legal division is responsible for acquiring permission for building improvements.
9. It is highly probable that XYZ's new policy on standardizing parts nomenclature will affect your operation. For that reason, let me explain in some detail 1) why this policy was adopted, and 2) the long-range benefit it promises to offer the company.

Obviously, in set B, sentence 5 presents the bottom-line by requesting specific information of the reader. In set C, sentence 9 quickly alerts the reader that the information that follows is of great relevance and should be digested carefully. The other sentences merely provide background information.

Once you become adept at spotting bottom-line sentences, you can scrutinize your own letters and memos carefully to see if they are getting off on the right bottom-line foot.

Decide for yourself whether you need more practice. If so, try the following three sets of opening sentences. Pick out the bottom line in each set.

Set D

10. The enclosed blueprints were completed last February.

11. As you requested in your letter of October 21, 198–, and our telephone conversation today, I've enclosed three blueprints of preliminary building layouts for your consideration.

12. We submitted blueprints of the original layout on March 15.

Set E

13. Material costs now comprise 40 percent of the sales value of our product.

14. Some companies have proposed combining Production, Control, Purchasing, and Distribution into a single Materials Management department.

15. Please ask your staff to conduct an in-depth evaluation of our current materials organization and recommend changes that will improve our ability to control materials costs.

Set F

16. Please seriously consider making some personnel available for transfer on a permanent or temporary basis.

17. There are currently 2,336 people employed in this division.

18. The division office provides estimates of the cost of right-of-way, relocation assistance, and appraisal fees, broken down on a tract-by-tract basis.

Clearly, sentences 11, 15, and 16 are the ones that effectively answer the "So what?" question.

FINDING THE BOTTOM LINE IN LONGER PASSAGES

Once you become adept at identifying bottom-line sentences, you'll be able to spot them readily in longer prose passages. Can you quickly spot the bottom-line sentence in the following?

I'd like to express my concern regarding one of our customers, Charles Rourke, owner and operator of Techtonics, Inc.

I continue to have difficulty collecting money he owes us for equipment delivered to his facilities. At present our records show three deliveries to Techtonics for which the firm owes us in excess of $5,000. Mr. Rourke has been billed monthly—since September—for this equipment, and I have talked to his assistant, Sheila Davis, by phone on three separate occasions. Ms. Davis claims Mr. Rourke travels a great deal, but she assures us he will pay us by the end of February.

I plan to continue to try to contact Mr. Rourke, requesting his cooperation in resolving this matter. Based on his past behavior, I recommend we take legal action against him.

Obviously, the final clause—"I recommend we take legal action against him"—is the bottom line. And everything else is meaningless until we come to this sentence.

Can you find the bottom line in this second passage?

The use of external consultants has been considered on several occasions.

In a memorandum dated October 25, 198–, XYZ issued guidelines for corporate use of external consultants. At that time, the company's first priority was getting internal consultants. Now we are genuinely concerned over the feasibility of finding external consultants to assist us in key areas.

Aside from two local consultants, headquarters has two objections to using externals for our purpose. First is data reliability. Headquarters contends that external consultants do not have as reliable data as internal consultants. The second is lack of specific expertise with XYZ, a problem that undercuts the validity of some of their suggestions. The attached memorandum provides statistical support for each of these objections.

It is our opinion that aggressively recruiting external consultants for XYZ would not be economically justified.

Again, the bottom line appears in the last sentence—"It is our opinion that aggressively recruiting external consultants for XYZ would not be economically justified."

Professional obfuscators have become remarkably adept at hiding bottom-line sentences in memos and reports. They hide them not just in closing sentences, but in middle paragraphs or, on some occasions, actually spread out in a number of different paragraphs. That is why veteran business readers have learned to scan entire reports, memos, or letters to spot the bottom line. Only in this way can they know whether a message requires close attention—or none!

Can you quickly spot the bottom-line sentence in this passage?

TO: XYZ HQ Managers

FROM: Purchasing Director

SUBJECT: Contact with Suppliers or Potential Suppliers

The XYZ policy on contacts with suppliers or potential suppliers is clearly outlined in the attached booklet, "Doing Business with Our Suppliers." All managers must recognize that when an employee's work requires oral or written communication with a supplier or potential supplier, authorization must be received from Purchasing prior to the employer contacting the supplier. This policy applies to employees' contacts relative to suppliers' or potential suppliers' commercial product lines as well as information, material, parts, equipment, services, and supplies.

This one is a little more difficult, isn't it? You notice, of course, that the bottom line is in the second sentence ("All managers must ..."). Furthermore, sentence 2 does not coherently follow sentence 1.

This memo would have been much clearer if the writer had begun with a proper bottom-line sentence like this:

Please obtain authorization from Purchasing when an employee's work requires oral or written communication with a supplier or potential supplier. This authorization must be received before the employee contacts the supplier.

Here's one that is even trickier. See if you can find the bottom line in this letter:

Dear Ms. Wood:

On June 5, 198–, I forwarded to you initial information on a book for the business trade market that we want copyrighted. The title of the manual is *Breaking in the Sales Force*.

This information was sent at your request so that you could begin preparing "appropriate assignment documents" for the copyrighting process. Since I have heard nothing from you for some time, I am writing to see if you need additional information. Please let me know the current copyright status of *Breaking in the Sales Force*.

Since I last corresponded with you, one of my colleagues has written a text entitled *Managing the Automated Office*. The full legal name of the author is John Paul Holmay. Please begin the copyright process on this text as well.

I appreciate the past work you have done for us and look forward to hearing from you.

If you are not careful you are apt to guess that the last sentence in the second paragraph is the entire bottom line. But if you read further, you will notice a second request is present—

"Please begin the copyright process on this text as well." Here is another example of a violation of bottom-line rule 2, which warns against scattering two or more purposes throughout a letter.

This is what should have been written:

Dear Ms. Wood:

This letter is to ask you to do two things:
1. Please let me know the current copyright status of *Breaking in the Sales Force.*
2. Please begin the copyrighting process for a book entitled *Managing the Automated Office,* written by my colleague John Paul Holmay.

If you have found the bottom-line sentences in all of the preceding passages you can rest assured that you can now find and recognize the bottom line in the vast majority of memos and letters that come across your desk. But just to ensure that you are an expert—and to give you an opportunity to redeem yourself if you answered any of the earlier examples incorrectly—let's look at one last letter. Can you find the bottom line in this letter, which we found in a corporate file?

R. H. Joyce
President, AB Diggers

Dear Bob:

Record keeping can no longer be a function performed at the discretion and convenience of the responsible party. The addition of part 48 to the federal law, coupled with the demands already imposed by parts 70, 75, and 77, has made accurate, timely records mandatory. We are now subject to MSHA audits with citations being issued for ill kept and inaccurate records.

Currently we are required to train in areas covered by state and federal laws, UMWA contracts, and company programs, and also participate in various outside programs. During 1980 we trained approximately 2,050 employees for a total of 16,700 hours. With this increasing demand for training, the trainers must utilize their time developing better methods, updating materials, and developing their own skills rather than recordkeeping. Presently they are spending five to six days per month on recordkeeping.

More and more demands are being placed on the already overloaded mine personnel supervisor. Currently he takes care of all personnel-related matters for 606 employees—98 salaried and 508 UMWA. A standard work week for this individual is 50–60 hours and approximately one-half of this time is devoted to reports and recordkeeping necessary to meet requirements of the various state and federal agencies, as well as our own needs. This activity includes all typing, filing, and clerical functions associated with maintaining a personnel office. With the many interruptions that are part of his daily functions, very little time is left to carry out and develop company programs that would be beneficial to the operation. Your consideration, approval, and assistance in providing us with an additional clerk position would be greatly appreciated.

I believe this change will allow both our trainers and the mine personnel supervisor the freedom and flexibility to develop programs that will directly affect and improve employee–employer relations and the safety, production, and efficiency of the operation.

Sincerely,

The length of the message—along with its ineffective organizational pattern—is this document's largest problem. If you are tired and tried to skim this message you probably missed the bottom line by assuming the message was merely informational. But in fact there is a bottom-line action request; unfortunately, it is hidden at the end of paragraph 3—"Your consideration, approval, and assistance in providing us with an additional clerk position would be greatly appreciated."

DEVELOP THE BOTTOM-LINE HABIT FOR EFFICIENCY

The ability to recognize a bottom-line sentence is the key ingredient in becoming a bottom-line writer. As you become proficient at identifying bottom lines in others' messages, you likewise become proficient in identifying them in your own. This will initially make revisions easier because once you know the bottom line you know how to organize your message. Eventually, the ability to recognize the bottom line will completely eliminate organizational revisions because you will develop the habit, before you write, of:

1. Determining what the bottom line is.
2. Deciding whether or not to state the bottom line at the beginning.

And once you reach this second stage you will have become an efficient writer, not only in terms of how you organize messages for your readers, but also in terms of a drastic reduction in the amount of time spent staring into space before you begin to write.

11

HOW TO WRITE
ACCEPTABLE FIRST-DRAFT
BOTTOM-LINE MESSAGES

Throughout this text we have shown how the rules of bottom-lining can be used to revise communications. We have shown an original memo or letter and then offered a bottom-line revision based on the application of one or more bottom-line rules.

But bottom-lining is more than just revision. It is a way of thinking through a situation *before* you write. It is a way of asking:

1. Why am I writing this message?
2. What is the best way for me to succeed?

As you learn to think in this way, you become more and more efficient at creating acceptable first drafts. And the amount of time you waste staring into space will shrink drastically.

The key to effective first drafts is to predetermine *why* you are writing; that is, what do you want to know, and what, if anything, do you want the reader to do? This does not mean that you will automatically state this information at the beginning of your message, for the situation may dictate otherwise. But it does mean that you will think through the situation in advance and determine for yourself where you want to place your bottom-line sentence.

You probably have noticed throughout this text a continuous emphasis on thinking, on predetermining what you are going to do. Bottom-lining and forethought go hand in hand; that is why good bottom-line writers seldom have problems with coherence. They logically determine the organization of their messages before writing by first identifying their bottom line and then deciding when to state it.

Let's take a typical business case and go through it step by step as we prepare to write a bottom-line answer to the situation.

Case 1

As aide to the president of a large oil firm, you are sent to a management–union meeting in a field superintendent's office. The meeting deals with an incident that occurred when two workers were involved in a collision with company equipment. The president tells you that he is worried the situation could get out of hand and that some major lawsuits and possible intervention from OSHA could occur unless an immediate resolution is achieved. You are asked to attend the meeting and report back to the president.

The meeting begins with an opening statement by the superintendent, Mike Bonner:

> The purpose of this meeting is to gather facts pertaining to the collision of Tony Simpson's bulldozer and Harry Land's steel hauler. Everyone will have an opportunity to state and explain the situation that occurred.

The remainder of the meeting involves testimony that is both confusing and inconsistent. Tony claims Harry accidentally bumped his dozer. Harry claims Tony hit his steel hauler. Tony claims his dozer was parked when Harry bumped it. Harry claims his hauler was parked when Tony hit it. A foreman claims there were hard feelings between Tony and Harry. Tony and Harry claim to be friends.

At the end of the meeting, Mike Bonner asks everyone to leave except for you, two managers, and two union negotiators. Mike then makes the following observations:

> It is hard to believe Tony and Harry, and I would like to discharge them both.

A union negotiator points out that since there was no witness to the accident, only Tony and Harry really know what happened. It would therefore be hard to prove that both deserved to be discharged. After some negotiation, the group agrees that Tony and Harry should both receive written reprimands and both should be suspended for ten days without pay.

Tony and Harry are brought in and agree to accept this punishment.

Before you write your report to the president, you decide to review your notes and think about the situation. Your big question, of course, is what is the bottom line? You arrive at the following possibilities:

1. The meeting achieved its stated purpose of giving witnesses the opportunity to explain what caused the August 19 collision of Tony Simpson's bulldozer with Harry Land's steel hauler.
2. The meeting showed that we can probably never determine what really happened in the collision.
3. The meeting was held, and a proposed reprimand and accompanying suspension have been agreed upon.

In truth, all three statements are legitimate bottom-line analyses of the meeting. Which one would you use?

Statement 1 was, obviously, the statement of the meeting's purpose as envisioned by Mike Bonner. And since bottom-lining and purpose go hand in hand, you might be tempted to use this as the bottom line of your message. But is this really the bottom line? Or was this really a kind of false purpose? Didn't the meeting go beyond this level? Wasn't more than factual information revealed?

Bottom-line statement 2 shows much of what was revealed. The statement offers a factual presentation of what occurred throughout much of the meeting. It even indicates the writer's frustration at being unable to sift out the true facts. Is this, then, the statement you would use?

One other consideration needs to be made, that of the reader. What does your president really want to know? The president sent you to report on what happened, but some of the "happenings" take precedence over others. Is the president really concerned that there are discrepancies in what is being reported? Does he care whether the bulldozer hit the steel hauler or the steel hauler hit the bulldozer?

This may concern a foreman or a superintendent, but the president cares about having the problem resolved with no further repercussions from the union or from outside inspectors.

The bottom line the president is concerned with is statement 3. The problem is resolved. No further action is necessary.

Once you have arrived at the relevant bottom line, the next question is fairly easy to answer: Where do you want to place the bottom line? Since the news of the resolution is pleasing to the reader, you should begin with a high-impact, bottom-line sentence stating that the problem was resolved.

But now what? You really have two options. First, you could offer a contract sentence summarizing how it was resolved and then proceed to fulfill your contract by giving the details. Or you could suggest that the details of how the resolution was reached are attached in an appendix, and then give a step-by-step description in the appendix. Of course, you realize that in fulfilling the contract sentence or in writing the appendix you are merely documenting the resolution and are providing useful information that will probably never be read since the president already knows as much as he wants to know.

Either of the following responses should do the job effectively and efficiently, and either could be produced in a first draft.

Response 1

The controversy over the incident involving the accident between the bulldozer and a steel hauler has been resolved. Management and union negotiators have agreed to impose a ten-day suspension on each employee and include a written reprimand in each employee's file.

This resolution was reached in a detailed meeting that involved:

1. Testimony from both employees involved in the incident.
2. Testimony from foremen who were at the scene but did not witness the incident.

A detailed explanation of the testimony follows.

Response 2

The controversy over the incident involving the accident between a bulldozer and a steel hauler has been resolved. Management and union negotiators have agreed to impose a ten-day suspension on each employee and include a written reprimand in each employee's file.

A detailed analysis of the meeting is attached.

HOW TO WRITE SUCCESSFUL FIRST DRAFTS IN PSYCHOLOGICALLY SENSITIVE SITUATIONS

As we have often mentioned, thinking your way through to the bottom line does not necessarily imply that you have found your beginning. There are other factors to consider, the most important being:

Is the bottom line psychologically sensitive?

In other words, will the reader have an emotional as well as a logical response to this message? If so, then you will want to consider two other questions:

1. What is my power relationship with the reader?
2. How will the reader react to the bottom line?

Once you have answered each of these questions, you can make your decision about where to place your bottom-line sentence. As you do, remember our earlier advice that all positive messages can be bottom-lined, as can negative messages downward, but negative messages upward deserve special consideration.

Let's try a couple of practice cases to see how these steps work.

Case 2

As state highway director, you receive a memo from Gladys Stevens, one of the Governor's top aides, regarding an outdoor advertising sign that a Reverend John Simpson uses for his local church. Reverend Simpson is under the impression that his sign is illegal and must be taken down as part of the Highway Beautification Act. The aide implies that you are picking on one of the governor's supporters and wants to know why, after the sign has been in existence for over ten years, it now has to be removed.

You research the problem and discover that one of your assistants wrote to Reverend Simpson and asked him not to remove the sign, but to obtain a permit for it. Reverend Simpson's church was not contacted about a permit until this year because the state route on which his church is located had a five-year grace period until the Beautification Act was to be enforced. The five-year period ended this year. The permit will cost Reverend Simpson $25.

What is the bottom line?

In this case, the bottom line is that Reverend Simpson does not have to remove his advertising sign, he merely has to get a permit for it.

What is your relationship to Ms. Stevens, the governor's aide?

You are in a politically appointed position as state highway director and your appointment came through the governor's office, so you are wise to regard her as a superior.

How will the reader perceive the bottom line?

Favorably. In fact, the aide probably will use it as an opportunity to show how the governor works for his constituents and twists some arms to get them favorable treatment.

With these thoughts in mind, which of the following beginnings do you prefer?

Response 1

This is in reply to your recent letter regarding correspondence you received from Reverend John Simpson relevant to an outdoor advertising sign belonging to the Colony Circle Church in Central City.

Response 2

I am pleased to be able to tell you that John Simpson's outdoor sign conforms with all federal highway requirements. All Reverend Simpson has to do is to obtain a permit for the sign. Let me explain the reasons for the issue relating to the outdoor sign.

Response 3

We do not feel that Reverend Simpson's church really has a problem. The location of the church sign is fortunate. Other individuals in organizations have not been so fortunate in terms of location. Let me explain this in more detail.

Obviously, response 1 violates the premise of bottom-lining. It offers background and beats around the bush, giving no specific indication of where the message is going. Response 3, on the other hand, disguises what should be clear. It implies Reverend Simpson is not violating the law, but it never directly states this. This situation is a pleasant one and you are writing to a superior, so you might as well gain maximum benefits from the situation by writing something like response 2.

Let's try a slightly more difficult case.

Case 3

At a recent staff meeting, Jane Johnson, the president of XYZ Company, indicated she is strongly considering laying off 10 percent of the nonexempt work force. Her goal, she said, is to benefit the profit-and-loss statement by offsetting lower sales revenue with lower production costs. The economy, her sources tell her, will continue to be depressed for at least another year. She therefore feels these drastic actions are needed.

This news of a layoff came upon you rather unexpectedly. As director of personnel research, you are not at all sure that this is the wisest path to follow. Because you had no solid factual data at the meeting with which to dispute Ms. Johnson's recommendations, you decided to remain silent and return to the office to check your data.

You have done so and your preliminary findings are that layoffs are not the wisest course for XYZ Company. But you need time to study the problem in more detail. Ms. Johnson will be returning from a business trip next month, at the same time you will be leaving on one. You therefore have to write a memo asking her to postpone her decision.

Will you bottom-line this report? Obviously, the gist of this communication is as follows:

1. *Bottom line:* Please place an immediate hold on your decision to lay off 10 percent of the nonexempt work force.
2. *Relationship to reader:* Reader is superior.
3. *Type of Message:* Negative/persuasive.
4. *Reader's likely response to message:* Negative.

With this information in mind, let's try a couple of potential beginnings. First, here's a well-written, bottom-line approach.

Version A

I recommend that you place an immediate hold on your decision to lay off 10 percent of the nonexempt work force. This hold will give my staff and me an opportunity to evaluate short-run versus long-run consequences of your recommendation that we preserve profits by cutting costs dramatically.

What do you think of this? It is bottom-lined, isn't it? But would you really want to be this direct in a negative message to your superior? In most instances—and certainly in this instance—probably not.

Let's try to blunt the impact a bit by keeping our sentences punchy but moving the bottom line to the end of the first paragraph. Does this do the job more effectively?

Version B

Yesterday I received your suggestion that we try to preserve profits by cutting labor costs dramatically. Although I agree with the goal of holding down costs, I think we need to evaluate the short-run versus long-run consequences of achieving this goal through cutting our factor work force. I am therefore asking you to put a hold on your layoff decision so that my staff and I can examine the effects of this decision.

This version is preferable to version A. But it might be a little too punchy. You may want to choose between the above version and a totally circuitous version like version C.

Version C

I endorse the goal of holding down costs you set forth at Friday's meeting. Such moves are of use not only in a recession, but also at times of prosperity. As I thought about your statements and your proposed actions, a number of auxiliary considerations came to mind. I feel I need to share these with you before you finalize your decision.

(Paragraphs 2, 3, and so on, would offer the qualifications.)

I hope you will agree with me that these are some serious considerations. Many of them need additional study. If it is possible, I would like to have my staff study these questions to see if we can get some more specific data for you before you make your decision.

I am, therefore, requesting that you give us an opportunity to study these problems in greater detail by temporarily withholding your decision to lay off 10% of the nonexempt work force. We have taken preliminary steps to begin a detailed study for you, if you so desire. We are, of course, at your service and would appreciate and look forward to hearing your response to our request.

Obviously, the circuitous pattern runs the risk of seeming to beat around the bush or of trying to manipulate the reader. But if it is carefully handled, especially in negative situations written upward, it can be the most effective. Whether you would choose version B or version C depends on a number of external factors, including your relationship with your boss and your boss's personality. But either approach would, we think, be preferable to that of a direct, punchy, bottom-lined version.

WRITING DOWN WITH SENSITIVITY

Let's reverse the two situations, requiring us to write down instead of up. How would you organize messages in this changed power position?

Case 4

Assume that you are Ms. Gladys Stevens, aide to the governor. You have just learned from Joe Harrington, the state highway director, that the outdoor advertising sign belonging to Colony Circle Church in Central City is actually in compliance with the state law. All the minister, the Reverend John Simpson, has to do is pay $25 for a permit. What factors should Ms. Stevens consider as she prepares to write a letter for the Governor's signature?

1. Bottom line: You do not have to remove your sign. Just purchase a permit for $25.

2. Relationship to reader: Superior. A governor is by far more powerful than is a local pastor; however, the governor, as an elected official, should approach this situation with sensitivity.

3. Type of message: Positive.

4. Reader's likely response to message: Positive, except for having to pay $25.

Which of the following three versions do you prefer?

Version A

Dear Reverend Simpson:

This is in reply to your letter regarding the outdoor advertising sign for your church. The reason you were contacted about the permit is that the Highway Beautification Act, passed by Congress during Lyndon Johnson's administration, mandated that states control outdoor advertising adjacent to Federal Aid Primary and Interstate Highway routes. Churches were granted an exemption provided that their signs did not exceed 8 square feet in size.

Your church was not contacted relevant to this matter until this year because State Route 48 did not become part of the Federal Aid Primary system until five years ago. The law provides for a five-year grace period after a route becomes a part of the system before compliance with the provisions of the act is required.

Fortunately, your sign is located in a conforming area and can be permitted. All you have to do is obtain a permit for the sign in conformance with the law. You can obtain this permit by going to the state highway district office and filling out an application. The cost for the permit is $25.

Version B

Dear Reverend Simpson:

I am pleased to be able to tell you that your outdoor advertising sign conforms with all federal highway requirements. All that you have to do is to obtain a permit for the sign. This permit can be obtained by contacting the district highway office in Elba.

Let me explain what I did in an effort to find this information out for you. At the same time, let me explain the reasons you were contacted about this requirement and the reasons for the requirement ....

Version C

Dear Reverend Simpson:

For a $25 permit fee you will be able to keep your outdoor sign. The sign conforms with all federal highway requirements. Let me ....

By now you should have dismissed version A without reading further than the second sentence. By the time you complete this sentence you realize the letter is not bottom-lined, and you have obviously decided that it should be.

Versions B and C are both bottom-lined; but which of the two did you prefer?

As a Governor writing to his constituents, you most likely chose version B. Why? Because the $25 permit fee might be perceived as bad news. Thus, this information should be placed in a position of lower impact, either at the end of the first paragraph or later in the letter. Either of these positions would lessen the effect on the reader and achieve a more desirable response from the reader.

Let's try our other case in reverse.

Case 5

This time you are Jane Johnson, the president of XYZ. Bob Short, the director of personnel research, has recommended that you lay off 10 percent of the nonexempt work force. After a preliminary study of Bob's recommendations, you decide that some other factors need to be considered before a decision is made.

If you were the president, which of the two organizational patterns would you send?

Version A

I appreciate your suggestion that we try to preserve profits by cutting labor costs dramatically. Such moves are always helpful toward achieving our corporate goals. Let me share with you some of my thoughts about your recommendation.

Version B

I am putting a hold on your recommendation that we lay off 10 percent of the nonexempt work force. I am taking this action even though I strongly endorse your attempts at preserving corporate profits. However, before we take such drastic actions we need to evaluate some short-run versus long-run consequences. Let me list a number of items I want your staff to study before we proceed with your suggestions.

Obviously, a number of factors influence which approach you prefer. But, as a general rule, the second, more direct approach seems more consistent with the president's role. Version A's circuitous approach, while possibly being interpreted as sensitive to the reader's concerns, runs the risk of making the president seem like a spineless bureaucrat.

IV

ESTABLISHING
A BOTTOM-LINE CLINIC
TO SAVE YOUR TIME
AND YOUR COMPANY'S
MONEY

12

GUIDELINES
FOR YOUR OWN
BOTTOM-LINE CLINIC

Will the concept of bottom-line reporting fill a real business need in your organization? We think so. If you agree with us, then the time for you to begin implementing the program is now, before people waste countless hours and dollars on inefficient, nonproductive memos and letters.

But, you ask, "Is it worth my time? What benefit does it have for me? Will a bottom-line program make a difference? What can I do?"

Based on our experience we can answer unequivocally yes to each of the first three questions. If you are inundated daily with numerous, foolishly written circuitous memos, then you have to take steps to correct the problem. You have to spread the bottom-line word to subordinates and, whenever possible, to superiors.

SPREAD THE BOTTOM-LINE WORD
THROUGH A BOTTOM-LINE CLINIC

A bottom-line clinic is nothing more than a group of fellow workers who meet to analyze the memos, letters, and other communications being sent within their organization. This analysis concentrates on when and where writers place ideas in a message and on how the writers could have done the job more efficiently and effectively. Although some attention should be paid to what is said—is the message positive, negative, or persuasive?—primary emphasis must be on when, where, and how. In other words, participants discuss whether or not an idea needs to be bottom-lined, not whether an idea was a wise managerial decision.

WHAT YOU NEED TO OPERATE THE CLINIC

All you need to begin a bottom-line clinic is a reasonable number of willing colleagues—somewhere between five and ten—and a room with chairs, tables, overhead projectors, and other basic audiovisual equipment.

Before each clinic session, designate one person as coordinator. The coordinator collects sample memos and letters from persons planning to attend. The coordinator asks for samples of some length—at least three-quarters of a page—and substance (no informal notes saying "I will be out of town next week").

After collecting the materials, the coordinator selects messages that either:

1. Need bottom-lining,
2. Need consideration as to whether bottom-lining is appropriate, or
3. Have buried or obscure action requests.

The coordinator then randomly distributes the messages into two stacks (labeled A and B) with six or seven memos in each stack and makes two overhead transparencies of each memo in each stack.

The actual clinic operates as follows:

1. Before the first meeting, participants must read this book. It has served as an excellent vehicle for discussion in many training programs we have run.

2. After participants acquire a firm grasp of the bottom-line concept, they break into small work groups. Each work group takes a prearranged packet of overhead transparencies (A or B) and goes to a breakout room. Each group writes new bottom-line beginnings for the memos in the packet. Participants write these beginnings on blank overhead transparencies.

3. After completing the assignment, participants return to the meeting room and display their new beginnings. Having groups work on the same memos and display their beginnings together is a particularly effective strategy. This format permits a comparison of beginnings and stimulates discussion of the organizational patterns used.

CLINIC WRAPUP

We suggest you end each clinic with a discussion of why businesspeople fail to bottom-line. Questions to help are:

- "What is the reason why so very few (almost no) on-the-job writers bottom-line their communications?"
- "Why do even short memos contain useless, time-wasting paragraphs?"
- "Why don't most people simply come to the point?"

The answer to all these questions, you will find, is basically this: Longwinded insecurity masquerading as thoroughness is rampant in business organizations.

INSECURITY MASQUERADING AS THOROUGHNESS

Since insecurity—and, to a degree, anxiety—are the primary motivators of unnecessarily long memos and reports written by subordinates, colleagues need to explore some of the common myths held by subordinates as they write upward in an organization:

1. "The more important my reader is, the more thorough and detailed my report needs to be."
2. "If I don't tell everything I know about the topic, my reader will be annoyed at having to request more information."
3. "The reader is not going to agree with me; I just know it! So I'll have to marshall and present all my evidence."
4. "This is my chance to show my superior how thorough, conscientious, and hardworking I am."
5. "The less certain I am, the more I need to write in order to sound convincing."

Coordinators should even distribute a list of these myths and encourage participants to post it somewhere in their offices. Writers can check themselves to see if they are not bottom-lining for some erroneous reasons.

But coordinators should be quick to note that these insecurity-based myths did not come out of the blue. Though not always secure, subordinates are seldom psychotic. Many of these writing insecurities stem from a real—not imagined—failure by superiors to communicate clearly and unequivocally their willingness to accept bottom-lined messages from subordinates.

Superiors need to be persuaded to tape the following credo to their walls:

1. I will recognize and appreciate subordinates' attempts to conserve my time in all memos and reports they write to me.
2. I will work out with subordinates some general understanding of how much detail I require in various circumstances.
3. I will make clear to subordinates that I judge their communications not by length and weight, but by their succinctness and crispness.
4. I will not become angry when subordinates bottom-line their thoughts to me—even when those thoughts are counter to mine.

Finally, subordinates should tape the following pledges to their office walls:

1. I will have the courage in all but the most sensitive or negative situations to bottom-line my purpose in writing, exactly what information I am trying to convey, and/or precisely what action I want my reader to take.
2. I will always bear in mind that my readers—especially if they are my superiors—are extremely busy. I will not waste their time by making

them read unnecessary or undigested detail—any more than I would waste their time chattering on in a face-to-face interview.

3. I will make a judgment about how much information my readers need to know in order to take the action required by the communication.

4. If I am in doubt about whether specific information is necessary to my readers, I will either put this information in summary form or in attachments, or tell readers that I stand ready to offer more information if so requested.

If all writers learned to hold and respond to these assumptions, longwinded, tediously boring messages would go the way of smallpox. And literally millions of corporate dollars would go back where they belong, into productive work and meaningful, honest, and tactful communications. The time to begin is now.

REVIEW OF BOTTOM-LINE RULES

Bottom-Line Rule 1:   State your purpose first unless there are overriding reasons for not doing so.

Bottom-Line Rule 2:   If there is more than one purpose to a communication, state both purposes at the beginning, or write two memos.

Bottom-Line Rule 3:   State your purpose first, even if you know your readers need a briefing before they can fully understand the purpose of your communication.

Bottom-Line Rule 4:   Always high-impact an action request—and bottom-line it if appropriate.

Bottom-Line Rule 5:   Bottom-line information in order of its importance to the reader.

Bottom-Line Rule 6:   Put information of dubious utility or questionable importance to the reader into an appendix. (This also applies to detailed information that probably will not be read in its entirety by the recipient.)

Bottom-Line Rule 7:   Never keep secret from the reader (or yourself) the direction(s) in which a complicated analytical discussion will go. Make a contract with your readers and fulfill every clause of that contract in the same sequential order as contracted.

Bottom-Line Rule 8:   In complex, multisectioned reports, write contract sentences for each subsection that:
1. Bottom-line what that subsection is about.
2. Make a transition from previous subsections to the present subsection (if needed).

3. Specify clearly the topics to be discussed in that subsection.

Bottom-Line Rule 9:

Always bottom-line the good news; there is no conflict between bottom-lining and positive messages.

Bottom-Line Rule 10:

In persuasive situations, where you do not know how your reader will react to what you ask for, bottom-line your request in all cases except:

1. Those in which you don't (or barely) know the reader, and to ask something immediately of a relative (or absolute) stranger would probably be perceived as "pushy."
2. Those in which the relationship between you and your reader is not close or warm.

Bottom-Line Rule 11:

Bottom-line downward negative messages unless extenuating circumstances are involved.

Bottom-Line Rule 12:

Think twice before bottom-lining negative messages upward.

Bottom-Line Rule 13:

Use a circuitous organizational pattern in negative requests written to persons in higher power positions, but still high-impact your action request.

APPENDIX ILLUSTRATIONS

Our experience indicates that the two best ways to learn to write are:

1. To recognize and understand the methodology being applied to situations.
2. To see examples or illustrations of what happens when such a methodology is applied.

The following illustrations exemplify the end product that emerges when bottom-line rules are applied to on-the-job memos.

We have classified these illustrations into the following two categories, each of which will be examined in Appendix A and B.

Appendix A: Bottom-Line Illustrations

A. How to Bottom-Line Informational Messages
B. How to Bottom-Line Positive Messages
C. How to Bottom-Line Negative Messages
D. How to Bottom-Line Persuasive Messages

Appendix B: Circuitous Illustrations

A. How to Make Persuasive Messages Circuitous
B. How to Make Negative Messages Circuitous

The examples in each section are accompanied by sparse, bottom-line analyses of the strategies used in each memo. By reading the description and studying the illustrations, you should be able to hone and refine your bottom-line skills to perfection.

APPENDIX A

BOTTOM-LINE ILLUSTRATIONS

HOW TO BOTTOM-LINE INFORMATIONAL MESSAGES

The five examples given here are typical of many of the messages sent throughout U.S. corporations. The messages are of a nonsensitive, informational type.

Basically, these five messages show you ways of transmitting information from one source to another when no outside barriers, such as emotions, power positions, and so on, are involved.

Message A

Message A is a sample cover letter that could accompany any kind of longer document. The letter begins by subtly persuading the reader (through the use of terms like "improve your XYZ subsystem," "improve response time," and "insure ease of growth") at least to read the cover letter.

Key suggestions are presented in an itemized format to make them as clear and direct as possible. After examining the cover letter, readers know 1) what the attached document is about, and 2) how thoroughly, if at all, they need to read it.

The bottom-line rules applied are:

> BOTTOM-LINE RULE 1: STATE YOUR PURPOSE FIRST UN-
> LESS THERE ARE OVERRIDING
> REASONS FOR NOT DOING SO.
>
> BOTTOM-LINE RULE 5: BOTTOM-LINE INFORMATION IN
> ORDER OF ITS IMPORTANCE TO
> THE READER.
>
> BOTTOM-LINE RULE 6: PUT INFORMATION OF DUBIOUS
> UTILITY OR QUESTIONABLE IM-
> PORTANCE TO THE READER INTO
> AN APPENDIX. (THIS ALSO AP-
> PLIES TO DETAILED INFORMA-
> TION THAT PROBABLY WILL NOT
> BE READ IN ITS ENTIRETY BY THE
> RECIPIENT.)

December 15, 19—

D. A. White
DP Manager
G & P Corporation
Government Product Division

Dear Mr. White:

I have enclosed information to help you improve your XYZ
subsystem. The objective of this information is to share some
thoughts that will improve response time in your system and
insure ease of growth.

In a nutshell, the basic suggestions are that you:

1. Review the data base and programming standards.
2. Establish a master terminal operator.
3. Establish performance monitoring.

Implementation of these suggestions should significantly improve
your operations.

I am available for any additional information or advice on the
subject.

Sincerely,

J. Daniel Frump

Message B

Here is a straightforward, clear, informational memo. Its purpose is to make way for additional information on what could possibly become a sensitive topic.

Specifically notice how this memo:

1. Begins with a bottom-line statement.
2. Explains briefly the reasons for the bottom line.
3. Offers a contract sentence of what is to follow.
4. Organizes the internal information numerically.

The bottom-line rules applied are:

BOTTOM-LINE RULE 1: STATE YOUR PURPOSE FIRST UNLESS THERE ARE OVERRIDING REASONS FOR NOT DOING SO.

BOTTOM-LINE RULE 3: STATE YOUR PURPOSE FIRST, EVEN IF YOU KNOW YOUR READERS NEED A BRIEFING BEFORE THEY CAN FULLY UNDERSTAND THE PURPOSE OF YOUR COMMUNICATION.

BOTTOM-LINE RULE 7: NEVER KEEP SECRET FROM THE READER (OR YOURSELF) THE DIRECTION(S) IN WHICH A COMPLICATED ANALYTICAL DISCUSSION WILL GO. MAKE A CONTRACT WITH YOUR READERS AND FULFILL EVERY CLAUSE OF THAT CONTRACT, IN THE SAME SEQUENTIAL ORDER AS CONTRACTED.

MEMORANDUM

DATE: April 15, 19—

TO: All Supervisors

FROM: Carlanda Ritter

SUBJECT: Individual Performance Goals and Objectives

Over the next two months we are going to ask all supervisors to formulate individual working objectives for each of their employees. These objectives will ensure that each Employee Performance Evaluation accurately reflects the employee's performance expectations.

A more detailed description of how the plan works will be sent later. For now, let me briefly give you an informative overview of what we plan to do.

First, each supervisor will meet with his or her employees and formulate performance objectives for each employee. These objectives will be made during our Employment Performance Evaluation. The performance objectives will be mutually agreed upon by the supervisor and the employee.

Second, supervisors and employees will review the objectives on a quarterly and on a semiannual basis. If an employee recognizes that he or she cannot meet a stated objective, the employee has the responsibility to inform the supervisor of this discovery at the earliest time possible. If the supervisor decides a renegotiation of objectives is necessary, he or she can conduct one.

Third, the performance review of objectives will be the basis for the annual performance evaluation. Once the system is implemented, supervisors and employees should have a solid foundation upon which to conduct the annual performance evaluation.

Message C

Here is a no-nonsense, straightforward quarterly report. Obviously, this writer is reporting nonsensitive, unemotional material.

Since the key to this kind of message is speed and efficiency, the writer begins with the bottom line and presents all of the message's ideas in a clear, simple format. Notice how the writer—through the use of asterisks—is able to designate for the reader the points of special importance.

The bottom-line rules applied are:

BOTTOM-LINE RULE 1: STATE YOUR PURPOSE FIRST UN-
LESS THERE ARE OVERRIDING
REASONS FOR NOT DOING SO.

BOTTOM-LINE RULE 5: BOTTOM-LINE INFORMATION IN
ORDER OF ITS IMPORTANCE TO
THE READER.

XYZ Oil
INTEROFFICE CORRESPONDENCE
Labor Relations

August 18, 19—

TO: Betty Stoner

RE: Labor Relations/Management Training Calendar

The attached calendar itemizes my expected activities for the
balance of 19—. Some of the activities need further explanation or,
in some cases, your assistance. Those requiring your assistance are
highlighted by an asterisk.

1. *10/5 Visit all work locations at XYZ.*
   I plan to visit every work site, meet as many employees as
   possible, and develop a good feel for every classification of
   work being done on our property. I will arrange to do this
   through John Holmes.

2. *10/15 Visit Consolidated Resources.*
   Ed Burns recommends I visit Consolidated for the purpose
   of setting up and organizing labor files. I will contact Ellen
   Richards (Consolidated) and arrange this.

*3. *11/10 Develop a Finite Labor and Training Plan.*
   It is important that you, John Holmes, Mark Wiggins, Joan
   Burke, and I meet to discuss the Labor and Training
   functions, reporting relationships, use of facilities, training
   needs and schedules, and so on.
   We should probably do this the week I report to work at
   AB #1.

*4. *11/15 Conduct Labor Training.*
   We had previously discussed not scheduling management
   training this fall. However, it could be advantageous to do
   so. I would establish my role more quickly, and the
   personnel would benefit immediately from training. Let's
   talk about this before the first of November.

5. *11/20 Plan 19— Objectives.*
   I am anticipating that you will want written objectives for
   19—.

6. *12/28 Schedule 19—, Report 19— Results.*
   I'll plan to schedule 19— training activities during this week
   as well as report 19— Labor and Training results.

Message D

This memo pushes bottom-line reporting to its extreme. All the material reported is organized and transmitted in as succinct a fashion as possible. This approach is effective for certain nonsensitive information.

Be careful of overusing bottom-line formats like this one. Such an approach is fine when it occurs between people who trust each other and who have no sensitive issues to discuss. In other words, this approach suits an uneventful quarterly report. Such an approach would, however, be ineffective and damaging if used at the wrong time or in the wrong situation.

The bottom-line rules applied are:

BOTTOM-LINE RULE 1: STATE YOUR PURPOSE FIRST UN-
LESS THERE ARE OVERRIDING
REASONS FOR NOT DOING SO.

BOTTOM-LINE RULE 5: BOTTOM-LINE INFORMATION IN
ORDER OF ITS IMPORTANCE TO
THE READER.

INTEROFFICE MEMO

ABC Energy Company
Safety Department

September 30, 19—

TO: Albert Lavor
          Administrator of Personnel

FROM: Bill Alfred
          Safety Trainer

SUBJECT: Quarterly Report

My activities for the past quarter and my objectives for next quarter are listed below:

1. Accomplishments for the quarter:
   1. Held mandatory training classes for 282 underground employees and 30 surface employees.

2. Worked at strip pit while Joe Feller was in National
  Guard.
3. Continued to visit shop, washer, and underground sections
  before and after having employees in class.
4. Attended Mine Rescue Contest in Pittsburgh.

2. *Reasons why objectives were or were not met:*
  All of my objectives, except orientation for new hires, were
  met for the quarter. We did not have any new hires.

3. *Objectives for the fourth quarter:*
  1. Hold eight-hour annual retraining class for remaining
    employees.
  2. Continue weekly site visits.
  3. Attend EMS Seminar at The University of Pittsburgh.

4. *Problems encountered or anticipated:*
  No problems encountered or anticipated.

5. *Program development status:*
  Continue to visit underground and surface facilities before
  and after classes. Also, continue to make slides—to be
  used in classes—of these areas.

6. *Overtime, if necessary, to accomplish objectives:*
  No overtime has been necessary.

Message E

Here is an excellent example of how to bottom-line a longer
document. After a one-sentence explanation of the reason for
writing, the writer goes directly to the bottom line, in this case a
recommendation.

The bottom-line sentence is followed by a contract sentence
that commits the writer and the reader to the internal organization of the remainder of the memo. The remaining information
is conveyed in as clear and direct a manner as possible.

The bottom-line rules applied are:

BOTTOM-LINE RULE 1: STATE YOUR PURPOSE FIRST UN-
LESS THERE ARE OVERRIDING
REASONS FOR NOT DOING SO.

BOTTOM-LINE RULE 5: BOTTOM-LINE INFORMATION IN
ORDER OF ITS IMPORTANCE TO
THE READER.

BOTTOM-LINE RULE 7: NEVER KEEP SECRET FROM THE
READER (OR YOURSELF) THE
DIRECTION(S) IN WHICH A COM-
PLICATED ANALYTICAL DISCUS-

SION WILL GO. MAKE A
CONTRACT WITH YOUR READ-
ERS AND FULFILL EVERY CLAUSE
OF THAT CONTRACT, IN THE
SAME SEQUENTIAL ORDER AS
CONTRACTED.

TO: A. J. Jacobs

FROM: S. B. Barlow

SUBJECT: Group Recommendation for Middle Management
              School

REFERENCE: T. W. Stahl's letter to you, dated February 25, 19—

Ben Burke and Tom Smith reviewed the proposal for a new
Group Middle Management School with me last week. Since our
current program is under way and funded, I recommend that we
not accept the changes for the current fiscal year. However, we
should be willing to consider the proposal carefully for the
upcoming year.

First, let me summarize my analysis of the proposal. Then I will
offer specific advantages and disadvantages of the present
proposal.

Summary
  • The proposal is a compromise between Group having its
    Middle Management School and XYZ maintaining its school.
    Under the plan each would have a one-week program, back to
    back.
  • There are more advantages to the rest of the Group than to
    XYZ from merging our school with theirs.

Pros
  • The presentation of the Group Mission might be better
    covered when developed and presented by the Group Staff.
  • Budgets would rise because of:
    1. Individual student enrollment.
    2. Support of a large Management Development Staff at
       Group.
  • Theoretically, the curriculum could be improved if a large
    number of Management Development instructors are brought
    together at the Group Staff.
  • Classes attended by individuals from different divisions do
    provide advantages from a cross-fertilization standpoint.
    Attitudes and philosophies of individuals in different divisions
    become evident during class discussions and case studies.

Cons
- XYZ would lose an element of control regarding:
  1. The curriculum and subjects presented.
  2. The assurance of being able to enroll as many people as we want in each class.
- As to curriculum, it might be awkward in making the cutover from the first week's session by Group Staff to the AB sessions during the second week. The program would require two different staffs, one for the first week and another for the second.

HOW TO BOTTOM-LINE POSITIVE MESSAGES

These five messages provide examples of positive messages that are bottom-lined. Examples range from short thank-you letters, to longer letters, to messages that simply convey good news. Any of the messages could serve as a prototype for various positive situations.

Message A

Here is an example of how to express sincere appreciation to a variety of people. Pay special attention to three facets of the organization of this memo:

1. The message begins with a broad-based thank-you. Everyone is set at ease.
2. The second paragraph demonstrates that the writer understood the difficulties the personnel worked under.
3. The third paragraph cites the accomplishments of two specific people. If the writer began with this praise and then offered general praise for everyone, the other readers would feel as if they were merely additions to the praise.

The length of this message is a bit excessive. Such length is appropriate for special cases of appreciation but would not be appropriate for the vast majority of such situations.

Bottom-line rules applied:

> BOTTOM-LINE RULE 1: STATE YOUR PURPOSE FIRST UNLESS THERE ARE OVERRIDING REASONS FOR NOT DOING SO.

> BOTTOM-LINE RULE 9: ALWAYS BOTTOM-LINE THE
> GOOD NEWS; THERE IS NO CON-
> FLICT BETWEEN BOTTOM-LINING
> AND POSITIVE MESSAGES.

MEMORANDUM

TO: All Supervisory Personnel

FROM: Martha Hartley
       Director

Please express my thanks and appreciation to all members of the Consultation staff for the dedication they have shown. The wonderful attitude maintained, the cooperation exhibited among the staff, and the days, weeks, and months of constant strain, effort, *and accomplishments* that took place during the reorganization have been most impressive.

We accomplished everything we set out to do despite ongoing training and new regulations and procedures. At the same time, you handled all jobs in an efficient, timely manner and thereby never sacrificed service to our customers.

I especially want to express appreciation to Brigitte Compton and Iris Terry, who so ably and efficiently served as Acting Supervisors during the period while the supervisor position was vacant. Both are to be commended for their capable and untiring efforts.

I thank you *all* for a job well done during this implementation period.

Message B

Here's a pleasant, short thank-you note. The writer chooses to stress:

1. Appreciation to each reader.
2. Acknowledgment that a particular plan is being implemented successfully.

Because of its brevity, this message provides a prototype for the vast majority of appreciation letters. It says:

1. Thanks.
2. All's going well.
3. Thanks again.

Bottom-line rules applied:

BOTTOM-LINE RULE 1: STATE YOUR PURPOSE FIRST UN-
LESS THERE ARE OVERRIDING
REASONS FOR NOT DOING SO.

BOTTOM-LINE RULE 9: ALWAYS BOTTOM-LINE THE
GOOD NEWS; THERE IS NO CON-
FLICT BETWEEN BOTTOM-LINING
AND POSITIVE MESSAGES.

TO: Branch Personnel Managers

FROM: R. N. Hogan, Divisional Personnel Manager

I thank each of you for your personal interest and involvement in
the promotion of the XYZ Suggestion Plan. I am happy to report
that the level of improvement in suggestion activity demonstrated
in 198— is continuing in 198—.

Also of significance, the suggestion-processing times and backlog
both show improvement over the previous year. The above
improvements are the direct result of your strong support.

Message C

Here is a combination good-news message and action request.
The writer is asking for a service the reader wants to provide, so
the good news should dominate and be bottom-lined, as it is.

Note how the writer is careful to add qualifications *after* giving
the reader the good news. Also, the writer uses a contract
sentence in order to make sure the reader sees the stipulations.

By arranging the information in this pattern, the writer
increases the likelihood of success because the reader does not
want to lose what he or she is so close to having. In essence, the
writer dangles a carrot in front of the reader and then says,
"Here's what you must do to have it."

BOTTOM-LINE RULE 1: STATE YOUR PURPOSE FIRST UN-
LESS THERE ARE OVERRIDING
REASONS FOR NOT DOING SO.

BOTTOM-LINE RULE 3: STATE YOUR PURPOSE FIRST,
EVEN IF YOU KNOW YOUR READ-
ERS NEED A BRIEFING BEFORE
THEY CAN FULLY UNDERSTAND
THE PURPOSE OF YOUR
COMMUNICATION.

> BOTTOM-LINE RULE 7: NEVER KEEP SECRET FROM THE READER (OR YOURSELF) THE DIRECTION(S) IN WHICH A COMPLICATED ANALYTICAL DISCUSSION WILL GO. MAKE A CONTRACT WITH YOUR READERS AND FULFILL EVERY CLAUSE OF THAT CONTRACT, IN THE SAME SEQUENTIAL ORDER AS CONTRACTED.
>
> BOTTOM-LINE RULE 9: ALWAYS BOTTOM-LINE THE GOOD NEWS; THERE IS NO CONFLICT BETWEEN BOTTOM-LINING AND POSITIVE MESSAGES.

Jake Alden
XYZ Company
2121 South Court Drive
Los Angeles, CA 49899

Dear Mr. Alden:

We would like to give your electric typewriter repair service a three- to six-month trial. We would like the service to begin as of March 1, 198–.

During the trial period you will be responsible for servicing 68 typewriters situated in the Blair Building at 1001 Heath Drive, Arcon Executive Center. Let me 1) clarify my understanding of the terms of the agreement, and 2) establish a criterion for incoming service calls.

As I understand the agreement, your service technician will service one or more of our typewriters for $35 plus a $1 travel charge. This charge applies whenever the time spent is one hour or less. For service time over one hour, the hourly charge is prorated in quarters of an hour.

We would, however, like to add the stipulation that calls for service come only from Beth McMullen, Arcon's service coordinator. Beth will be our principal contact with your organization. *In order to exercise proper records for this trial period, please do not accept any calls for service unless such calls originate from Beth.*

After a suitable period, we will evaluate response time and quality of service rendered. If we find it satisfactory, we will consider your all-inclusive yearly service contract. If you are in agreement with the above terms, then please begin our service as of March 1.

I look forward to a long and mutually beneficial business relationship with your organization.

Sincerely yours,

J. S. Stone

Message D

A report on company safety standards can be a very threatening document. This cover letter demonstrates how to handle the situation when the company is in full compliance with the standards.

Notice how the writer, by beginning with the good news, removes all threat to the reader. The writer even documents the good news by citing highlights from the report.

The one slightly negative issue—new regulations—is broached in a very positive manner. The basic message is that the company needs minor, unimportant, inexpensive adjustments.

Finally, the letter ends personally with the consultant reaffirming the letter's positive nature. Many writers would be inclined to begin with such a thank-you but, by doing so, would impede the effectiveness of this message. Most readers of this kind of letter would probably regard an opening thank-you as a mere courtesy preceding some bad news.

Bottom-line rules applied:

BOTTOM-LINE RULE 1: STATE YOUR PURPOSE FIRST UNLESS THERE ARE OVERRIDING REASONS FOR NOT DOING SO.

BOTTOM-LINE RULE 3: STATE YOUR PURPOSE FIRST, EVEN IF YOU KNOW YOUR READERS NEED A BRIEFING BEFORE THEY CAN FULLY UNDERSTAND THE PURPOSE OF YOUR COMMUNICATION.

BOTTOM-LINE RULE 5: BOTTOM-LINE INFORMATION IN ORDER OF ITS IMPORTANCE TO THE READER.

BOTTOM-LINE RULE 9: ALWAYS BOTTOM-LINE THE GOOD NEWS; THERE IS NO CONFLICT BETWEEN BOTTOM-LINING AND POSITIVE MESSAGES.

Donald Astin
ABCD Corporation
115 Rhodes Street
Atlanta, GA 31301

Dear Mr. Astin:

The attached report on solvent levels and asbestos concentration
shows your firm is in compliance with all federal safety standards
for each of these areas.

The results of the survey indicate:

1. Solvent levels well below the eight-hour time-rated average
   allowed by federal regulations. Because levels are so low, only
   the results of the survey are included in this report.
2. Asbestos concentrations are also below the eight-hour time-
   rated average allowed by federal regulations.

Some new regulations regarding employees' handling of asbestos
will be forthcoming later this year. I have attached a copy of these
regulations since you will need to make some adaptations to them,
even though your concentrations are below federal standards.
These changes can be made with a minimum of effort and no
financial expenditures.

I personally thank you for your cooperation during the survey. If
you have any questions, or if we can be of any further assistance,
please call us.

Sincerely,

Alexis Anderson

Message E

The writer of this memo had two areas of emphasis to choose
from:

1. The closing of the building for electrical repairs.
2. The extra days off for clerical workers.

The writer wisely chose to emphasize point 2 and thereby was
able to maximize the positive benefits of this message.

Notice how the memo begins with the bottom line and then
follows by answering what will obviously be the key question

asked about the time off: "Will it count against our regular vacation time?" The answer is no.

Also notice how the writer maintains a lighthearted, friendly style and consistently focuses on the employee point of view. From a productivity point of view, the managerial writer may resent having to give clerical staff this extra vacation. But she shrewdly does not let this show through and thereby maximizes the positive impact of this extra vacation.

Bottom-line rules applied:

> BOTTOM-LINE RULE 1: STATE YOUR PURPOSE FIRST UN-LESS THERE ARE OVERRIDING REASONS FOR NOT DOING SO.
>
> BOTTOM-LINE RULE 5: BOTTOM-LINE INFORMATION IN ORDER OF ITS IMPORTANCE TO THE READER.
>
> BOTTOM-LINE RULE 9: ALWAYS BOTTOM-LINE THE GOOD NEWS: THERE IS NO CON-FLICT BETWEEN BOTTOM-LINING AND POSITIVE MESSAGES.

TO: Clerical Staff

FROM: Pat Jones

All clerical staff will receive three days of paid vacation from June 1 to June 3. This time will not count against sick leave nor against regular vacation time.

If heavy rains occur between May 31 and June 3, you might also have off June 4–5. We want to make sure you have a sunny vacation. Telephone operators will be available from 6 A.M. to 8 A.M. on the morning of June 4 to answer questions about this extension. No extension will be granted if the period between May 31 and June 3 is dry.

This unexpected—but well-earned—bonus vacation comes courtesy of Building Maintenance. As you may know, some necessary electrical repairs have been waiting in the wings for a long time. Power needs to be shut off throughout the building for Maintenance to be able to conduct the repairs.

The beginning of summer seemed like an excellent time to shut down the building. I'm sure you agree.

Have a nice bonus vacation.

HOW TO BOTTOM-LINE NEGATIVE MESSAGES

These five messages illustrate various ways to bottom-line negative messages. Although each example uses a bottom-line organizational pattern, the forcefulness of the particular samples ranges from "now hear this" types of orders to passively stated requests. Each example could serve as an excellent prototype for various negative situations.

Message A

This memo's purpose is to clarify job responsibilities—who is to do what. The writer uses a bottom-line organizational pattern but blunts the message's impact slightly by stating the bad news in a passive sentence. However, thanks to the direct organizational pattern, there is little or no chance that the reader will misunderstand what is being said.

Notice how the writer intentionally stays out of the memo. He states the bottom line passively, states the basis for making the decision, and then stops. No apologies or expressions of sympathy are included, probably to protect the writer from being accused of being for or against the stated policy. In essence, the reader can interpret the writer's feelings about this policy as the reader wishes; the writer offers no clue for an accurate interpretation.

Bottom-line rules applied:

BOTTOM-LINE RULE 1:	STATE YOUR PURPOSE FIRST UNLESS THERE ARE OVERRIDING REASONS FOR NOT DOING SO.
BOTTOM-LINE RULE 3:	STATE YOUR PURPOSE FIRST, EVEN IF YOU KNOW YOUR READERS NEED A BRIEFING BEFORE THEY CAN FULLY UNDERSTAND THE PURPOSE OF YOUR COMMUNICATION.
BOTTOM-LINE RULE 5:	BOTTOM-LINE INFORMATION IN ORDER OF ITS IMPORTANCE TO THE READER.
BOTTOM-LINE RULE 11:	BOTTOM-LINE DOWNWARD NEGATIVE MESSAGES UNLESS EXTENUATING CIRCUMSTANCES ARE INVOLVED.

DATE: March 4, 19—

TO: Joe Jones

FROM: Edward Parr, Employee Relations Director

SUBJECT: Inclement Weather Policy

It is necessary to charge you eight hours annual leave for last Wednesday's absence. Kathy Sumers, in the Office of Employee Assistance and Program Evaluation, clarified the policy.

If an employee does not come to work, he or she is to be charged with eight hours annual leave regardless of the time announced for closings. Those employees who come to work but then decide they want to leave early should be charged annual leave from the time they leave until the announced time of closing. (For example, if an employee decides to leave at 3 P.M. and the decision to close is made at 4 P.M., the employee will be charged with one hour annual leave.)

Message B

Here is a message that begins with a bottom-line recommendation. The bottom line is negative because the reader, a subordinate, wanted to continue using Mini-Center Stores as business outlets.

Regardless of the reader's preference, the writer presents the recommendation in a straightforward manner. She then follows with 1) a contract sentence to show how she will document her belief, and 2) the documentation. Obviously, this writer has complete confidence in the recommendation and in the reasons for it.

Bottom-line rules applied:

BOTTOM-LINE RULE 1:	STATE YOUR PURPOSE FIRST UNLESS THERE ARE OVERRIDING REASONS FOR NOT DOING SO.
BOTTOM-LINE RULE 5:	BOTTOM-LINE INFORMATION IN ORDER OF ITS IMPORTANCE TO THE READER.
BOTTOM-LINE RULE 7:	NEVER KEEP SECRET FROM THE READER (OR YOURSELF) THE DIRECTION(S) IN WHICH A COMPLICATED ANALYTICAL

> DISCUSSION WILL GO. MAKE A CONTRACT WITH YOUR READERS AND FULFILL EVERY CLAUSE OF THAT CONTRACT IN THE SAME SEQUENTIAL ORDER AS CONTRACTED.
>
> BOTTOM-LINE RULE 11: BOTTOM-LINE DOWNWARD NEGATIVE MESSAGES UNLESS EXTENUATING CIRCUMSTANCES ARE INVOLVED.

DATE: April 15, 19—

TO: Jack Sezar, Mini-Center Coordinator

FROM: Jane Thompson, Vice-President of Operations

SUBJECT: Business in Mini-Center Stores

We recommend that XYZ stop considering Mini-Center Stores as business outlets. The question of using Mini-Centers for business purposes has been pursued on several occasions, and the findings consistently show few opportunities. Let me briefly explain our reason for this recommendation

Aside from small business customer participation, our location people point to two objections to using Mini-Center Stores for business purposes. The first is space. Most stores do not currently have adequate space for center needs.

The second is the employees' lack of expertise with business customers. Mini-Center Store employees would have to be trained and kept up to date on business procedures, rates, and so on. Furthermore, XYZ files would need to begin containing business records, a time-consuming and expensive adjustment.

We can therefore see no economic justification for continuing to consider Mini-Center Stores as business outlets.

Message C

This memo does an effective job of communicating negative information in a bottom-line fashion. The writer avoids singling out individuals and instead says, "Let's clarify the responsibilities of those involved." The problem, which the writer treats briefly but clearly, is that some customers are having installation problems because the writer's company has not defined the customers' responsibilities nor given them proper guidance. In essence, there is confusion about who is to do what. This memo's purpose is to clarify responsibilities.

Notice that while this is a bottom-lined negative memo, it does not go so far as to antagonize or point a finger at specific groups. After announcing the problem, the writer says, "Here is each group's responsibility." The responsibilities are then presented in a clear, efficient fashion.

Bottom-line rules applied:

BOTTOM-LINE RULE 1:	STATE YOUR PURPOSE FIRST UNLESS THERE ARE OVERRIDING REASONS FOR NOT DOING SO.
BOTTOM-LINE RULE 8:	IN COMPLEX, MULTISECTIONED REPORTS, WRITE CONTRACT SENTENCES FOR EACH SUBSECTION THAT:
	1. BOTTOM-LINE WHAT THAT SUBSECTION IS ABOUT.
	2. MAKE A TRANSITION FROM PREVIOUS SUBSECTIONS TO THE PRESENT SUBSECTION (IF NEEDED).
	3. SPECIFY CLEARLY THE TOPICS TO BE DISCUSSED IN THAT SUBSECTION.
BOTTOM-LINE RULE 11:	BOTTOM-LINE DOWNWARD NEGATIVE MESSAGES UNLESS EXTENUATING CIRCUMSTANCES ARE INVOLVED.

DATE: January 1, 19—

TO: Support Engineers

FROM: J. J. Jones, Head of Support Services

SUBJECT: Customer Setup of New Abda Processors

The new Abda Processors have arrived in Trussville. Our customers, however, have mixed feelings about the new Customer Establish design. Those customers who were informed early of their responsibilities and given proper guidance have had few problems. Others have not been so fortunate. To assist the less fortunate, let's clarify the responsibilities of those involved.

Marketing personnel have overall responsibility to:

1. Inform each customer of his or her responsibility to set up the equipment.
2. Supervise the plan.

Support Engineers have responsibility to:

1. Review with the customer the detailed steps required for a successful installation.
2. Guide the customer in developing a plan for the installation.

The following tasks should assist Support Engineers in providing the appropriate help to their customers:

1. Carefully check the specifications, keyboards, and cables to assure that each matches customer requirements.
2. Review the Company Update articles that cover the new devices. I have copies of this material available for your use.
3. Inform your customers that the keyboards on the new display stations are considerably different from those on others. Acceptance of the new keyboards should be good if customers are instructed properly.
4. Plan for education. Personnel Training is available for only $30.00. In addition, the Demo Room is available for customer demonstrations. If given one week's notice, Nancy Brown or I can give this demonstration to your customer.

The attached planning checklist should be used to ensure that all areas of the installations have been covered.

If you have any questions, please contact Nancy or me as soon as possible.

Message D

Here is a bottom-lined "now hear this" type of memo. No employee will dare misunderstand the writer's message. The forcefulness of this memo, in terms of both organization and style, suggests that readers who violate these orders do so at their own risk.

Bottom-line rules applied:

BOTTOM-LINE RULE 1:	STATE YOUR PURPOSE FIRST UNLESS THERE ARE OVERRIDING REASONS FOR NOT DOING SO.
BOTTOM-LINE RULE 11:	BOTTOM-LINE DOWNWARD NEGATIVE MESSAGES UNLESS EXTENUATING CIRCUMSTANCES ARE INVOLVED.

MEMO:To Staff

RE: Break Room

FROM: Director

PLEASE observe the time in the mornings. You should be at your desks at 8:00 A.M.

Some staff members have been in the break room routinely past 8:00 A.M. If you are one of these persons, please watch the time. This also applies to 1:00 P.M.—being back on the job on a timely basis.

Be mindful of the 15-minute break limit. I feel sure we all have enough work to keep us fully occupied.

Thank you for your cooperation.

Message E

Though not as forceful as message D, this message still conveys its negative information in a bottom-line fashion. This writer: 1) acknowledges the reader's recommendation, 2) states the bottom line, and 3) offers a contract sentence stating that evidence for the writer's recommendation will be provided.

A receiver of message E has to be impressed by the certainty with which the writer approaches this topic. He or she obviously feels completely confident in the supporting information provided.

Bottom-line rules applied:

BOTTOM-LINE RULE 1:	STATE YOUR PURPOSE FIRST UNLESS THERE ARE OVERRIDING REASONS FOR NOT DOING SO.
BOTTOM-LINE RULE 3:	STATE YOUR PURPOSE FIRST, EVEN IF YOU KNOW YOUR READERS NEED A BRIEFING BEFORE THEY CAN FULLY UNDERSTAND THE PURPOSE OF YOUR COMMUNICATION.
BOTTOM-LINE RULE 7:	NEVER KEEP SECRET FROM THE READER (OR YOURSELF) THE DIRECTION(S) IN WHICH A COMPLICATED ANALYTICAL DISCUSSION WILL GO. MAKE A

> CONTRACT WITH YOUR READERS AND FULFILL EVERY CLAUSE OF THAT CONTRACT, IN THE SAME SEQUENTIAL ORDER AS CONTRACTED.
>
> BOTTOM-LINE RULE 11: BOTTOM-LINE DOWNWARD NEGATIVE MESSAGES UNLESS EXTENUATING CIRCUMSTANCES ARE INVOLVED.

TO: Site Manager

SUBJECT: Revision Reports

Rather than eliminating Revision Reports, as suggested by your memo, we in headquarters hold the opinion that Revision Reports should continue to be prepared. In fact, we strongly suggest that these reports be made more candid and therefore more useful.

Let me explain why we think these reports must be frank and hard-hitting. Thousands of dollars are invested each year in testing our products to ensure customer satisfaction. By not conducting product revisions, we would lose a major source of input on how we might better spend those dollars to enhance our evaluations. Furthermore, if the results of product revisions are not reported, potential gains are minimized.

The internal value of such revisions should be reflected in an ever-evolving set of evaluation techniques based on reactions to our customers' experiences with our products. Externally, such reports should help improve cross-location communications, pointing out common problems that could be addressed from a divisional perspective. Our roles are 1) as a center for testing of expertise for the division, and 2) as a service group to Development. Both roles stand to benefit from a comparison of product success to evaluation methods used.

As you can see, then, product revision reports are a valuable tool in helping us stay on top of our increasingly competitive market. We need to put this tool to its most effective use.

HOW TO BOTTOM-LINE PERSUASIVE MESSAGES

Here are six bottom-lined persuasive messages that can be used in a variety of situations. The first two exemplify requests sent downward from a superior to subordinates. The third is a recommendation letter that could be sent in any direction—up, down, or across. The final three are requests sent to superiors.

As you examine each message, notice how the amount and kind of documentation change based on the differing positions of the reader.

Message A

Here is an excellent example of a brief, bottom-lined persuasive request. After a half-sentence of background, the writer:

1. Makes her general request ("I ask that each of you").
2. States her specific requests in a high-impact, itemized, imperative manner.

Such an approach is efficient and useful if:

1. The writer has sufficient power or status to make such a direct request.
2. The readers have neutral (or positive) feelings toward the action being requested.

Bottom-line rules applied:

BOTTOM-LINE RULE 1: STATE YOUR PURPOSE FIRST UNLESS THERE ARE OVERRIDING REASONS FOR NOT DOING SO.

BOTTOM-LINE RULE 4: ALWAYS HIGH-IMPACT AN ACTION REQUEST AND BOTTOM-LINE IT IF APPROPRIATE.

TO: B. Loomis
F. Ryerson
J. Suchan

FROM: J. B. Mason

SUBJECT: Gasoline Shortage Contingency Planning

It is necessary for all divisions to conform to corporate policy requiring forty hours of training for each employee. Therefore:

1. Appoint one person from your division to monitor personnel adherence to this policy.
2. Ask this person to:
   a) Keep employees updated about educational offerings and

about the need of each employee to complete the
mandatory hours.
   b) Report quarterly on all matters pertinent to the effective
   implementation of this worth-while policy.
3. Periodically remind employees that we continue to provide
   them with assistance in locating others interested in carpooling.

Message B

Like message A, this message states its request directly and
immediately. Again, this message offers little documentation of
the reasons for the request.

As mentioned earlier, such an approach is acceptable for
nonsensitive messages sent down the chain of command.

Bottom-line rules applied:

BOTTOM-LINE RULE 1: STATE YOUR PURPOSE FIRST UN-
LESS THERE ARE OVERRIDING
REASONS FOR NOT DOING SO.

BOTTOM-LINE RULE 4: ALWAYS HIGH-IMPACT AN AC-
TION REQUEST AND BOTTOM-
LINE IT IF APPROPRIATE.

TO: J. H. Allen
       Ms. E. J. Jenkins
       Mr. J. J. Hopkins
       Ms. L. S. Stephens

FROM: Jean Giscard

Please encourage the managers whose names are listed on the
attachment to attend regularly the meeting of the Pension
Investment Board.

The next meeting will be held on Tuesday, March 20, from 9 to 12
in Conference Room 14–C, Building B. Please have your
representatives:

1. Contact Joyce Spinelli for any further information and to
   confirm his or her attendance.
2. Be prepared to discuss the investment plans submitted for
   review at the February 2 meeting.
3. Be ready to discuss other investment opportunities in the
   current economy.

Message C

Here is a non-threatening persuasive letter that gets the job done most efficiently. Following the bottom-line recommendation, the writer offers brief general praise, then a contract sentence for the remainder of the letter.

This letter needs to be long for a number of reasons. First, the case for Ms. Roberts is made most effectively by providing extensive, specific information. Second, the length demonstrates the writer's familiarity with Ms. Roberts. And, third, the length implies that the writer cares about Ms. Roberts and wants her to win the award.

Isn't this type of request much more effective than one that says, "Carol Roberts is the greatest person I have ever worked with," and then stops?

Bottom-line rules applied:

BOTTOM-LINE RULE 1: STATE YOUR PURPOSE FIRST UNLESS THERE ARE OVERRIDING REASONS FOR NOT DOING SO.

BOTTOM-LINE RULE 4: ALWAYS HIGH-IMPACT AN ACTION REQUEST AND BOTTOM-LINE IT IF APPROPRIATE.

BOTTOM-LINE RULE 5: BOTTOM-LINE INFORMATION IN ORDER OF ITS IMPORTANCE TO THE READER.

Dear Mr. Higgins:

I am writing to recommend Ms. Carol Roberts for XYZ's Excellence Award. Ms. Roberts has done an outstanding job for XYZ for a number of years, and this last year she exceeded all previous accomplishments. Let me elaborate on some of these accomplishments, especially those she most recently completed.

EIO/123

Most of Ms. Roberts' work last year centered on two major projects. The first, EIO/123, involved establishment of a new software package. Two of Ms. Roberts' particular achievements were:

   1. The development of an alternative pricing system based on variable cost slopes. This development increased XYZ's

revenue and profits and our improved competitive edge with this product.

2. The acceptance of responsibility for updating the EIO/123 system. This updating was completed in advance of the due date and at a cost lower than projected. In addition, the project met all quality control standards.

RSV/789

After completing the EIO/123 project, Ms. Roberts was assigned to the RSV/789 business guidance project. On this project she not only performed forecast cases for XYZ—each of which proved exceedingly accurate and significantly increased the quality of the end product—but she also made key suggestions regarding implementation recommendations. These latter suggestions led to significant cost reductions.

Also while working on this project, Ms. Roberts organized and put together a one-day program for XYZ field representatives. This program encouraged the representatives to push our products and probably contributed—more than any other factor—to sales being above anticipated margins.

Jim, Carol Roberts has worked for XYZ for 15 years. Every year she has done a better job than the last. I sincerely believe it's time we begin to recognize employees like Carol Roberts and give them their credit.

I hope you agree and will select her for XYZ's Excellence Award. I look forward to learning your decision.

Sincerely,

Message D

This message summarizes a longer, more detailed report. To make both the attached document and the cover letter easily accessible to the reader, the writer wisely begins with a bottom-line request.

Specifically, notice how the writer:

1. States the request as a question. Obviously, this softens the impact (and is appropriate with some superior readers).
2. Follows the request with a summary recommendation.

Each of the last two steps makes the information in the report easily accessible to a reader.

Bottom-line rules applied:

BOTTOM-LINE RULE 1: STATE YOUR PURPOSE FIRST UNLESS THERE ARE OVERRIDING REASONS FOR NOT DOING SO.
BOTTOM-LINE RULE 4: ALWAYS HIGH-IMPACT AN ACTION REQUEST AND BOTTOM-LINE IT IF APPROPRIATE.
BOTTOM-LINE RULE 6: PUT INFORMATION OF DUBIOUS UTILITY OR QUESTIONABLE IMPORTANCE TO THE READER INTO AN APPENDIX. (THIS ALSO APPLIES TO DETAILED INFORMATION THAT PROBABLY WILL NOT BE READ IN ITS ENTIRETY BY THE RECIPIENT.)

TO: A.J. Strickland

FROM: Morris Mayer

SUBJECT: New Facilities

Attached are the plans and sketches of the new Suburban Plaza branch office and a statement of whom it will house when it is ready for occupancy in an August/September time frame. Would you please consider this outline and let me know if my approach is in agreement with your thinking?

Notice that I suggest that we leave the downtown branch in its current location but provide it with additional space for expansion. I recommend that we move all other staff functions into the new building. This will minimize commuting time for most personnel.

Message E

This bottom-line request is sent not only to a superior, but to a benefactor. Yet, by being bottom-lined, the message acquires professional dignity and integrity. This writer neither grovels nor tries to be a huckster and con support from the reader.

Instead, the writer states directly and honestly:

1. Please continue helping us.
2. Your past help has been most valuable.
3. Here's what we've done, and here's what we plan to do.

As with message D, length here is an asset, not a detriment. Bottom-line rules applied:

> BOTTOM-LINE RULE 1: STATE YOUR PURPOSE FIRST UNLESS THERE ARE OVERRIDING REASONS FOR NOT DOING SO.
>
> BOTTOM-LINE RULE 4: ALWAYS HIGH-IMPACT AN ACTION REQUEST AND BOTTOM-LINE IT IF APPROPRIATE.
>
> BOTTOM-LINE RULE 7: NEVER KEEP SECRET FROM THE READER (OR YOURSELF) THE DIRECTION(S) IN WHICH A COMPLICATED ANALYTICAL DISCUSSION WILL GO. MAKE A CONTRACT WITH YOUR READERS AND FULFILL EVERY CLAUSE OF THAT CONTRACT IN THE SAME SEQUENTIAL ORDER AS CONTRACTED.

John Jones
AMT Incorporated
55 State Street
Anytown, AL 23456

Dear Mr. Jones:

I am writing to request a continuation of funding for the Urban Development Program. Your assistance has allowed us to make great strides in the past year. We plan to continue to advance in the direction we have started to follow. Let me elaborate on some of our most significant accomplishments and our future plans.

Day-Care Centers

During the past year we have established fourteen day-care centers throughout the city. Ten of these fourteen centers are located in low-income areas. In total, these day-care centers handle 512 children between the ages of one and five. Without these programs, these children might be abused, neglected, or abandoned.

Juvenile Youth Center

We have completed plans and begun operation of a Juvenile Youth Center. This operation, located at the corner of Fifteenth and Willshire Blvd., is in the heart of a high-crime area. The center has eight full-time counselors available to teens ranging in age from twelve to eighteen. In addition, a number of recreational facilities—including handball courts and a weight-lifting club—are open sixteen hours a day.

Although this center has only been open for two months, more than 800 inner city youths have passed through its doors already. If our current attendance rate continues to increase, we should soon see some significant behavior changes in the area surrounding the youth center.

Homes for the Elderly

A final project we have undertaken during this year is a kind of clearinghouse function for many of the elderly citizens of our city. We have established in our downtown center an office in which we try to find available homes for persons over 70 who need some personal care. We do not attempt to place those who are invalids.

The idea behind this program is to alleviate much of the crowding currently experienced in many of the area's nursing homes. Also, we try primarily to help those who cannot afford to be in these nursing homes.

So far this program has been most successful. We have placed 89 people in local residences and have a complaint rate of less than 10 percent. This rate is significantly lower than the national average of 28 percent.

Future Plans

Perhaps the most promising aspect of each of these programs is that the Urban Development Program is primarily concerned with establishing, not continuing, the programs described above. In other words, as we mentioned to you last year when we asked for your assistance, our goal is to set up well-run organizations. Once we have those organizations permanently in place, we then hope to either have them become self-perpetuating or to turn them over to local agencies for continuation. We will then withdraw from each of these agencies and serve only in a consulting capacity.

As you can see, we have taken a number of significant steps during the past year. We could not have taken these steps without your financial support. We hope that you approve what we have done with your help and that you will continue to support our programs by approving additional funding.

Message F

Here is another bottom-line request sent to a superior. The keys to its success are similar to those of the messages that preceded it:

1. A direct statement of the request.
2. Detailed documentation supporting the request.

Bottom-line rules applied:

> BOTTOM-LINE RULE 1: STATE YOUR PURPOSE FIRST UN-
> LESS THERE ARE OVERRIDING
> REASONS FOR NOT DOING SO.
>
> BOTTOM-LINE RULE 4: ALWAYS HIGH-IMPACT AN AC-
> TION REQUEST AND BOTTOM-
> LINE IT IF APPROPRIATE.

Dear Mr. Jones:

I am writing to request additional support personnel for the marketing area. Specifically, I would like to add:

1. Three members to the field staff.
2. Two members to the market research staff.
3. Two administrative staff assistants.

The current workload of the marketing staff is unwieldy, and I am afraid we will begin to provide inadequate service to XYZ's customers without additional support.

The following statistics support my requests:

Field Personnel

We presently have four members of our sales staff covering a five-state area with more than 200 customers. This area, our Southwestern Region, is experiencing tremendous growth—more than 25 percent per year for the last three years. As a result, field personnel has simply been unable to tap a number of new industries in the area. The addition of three field personnel members will not only improve the quality of service to our existing customers, but will also significantly expand the scope of our operations.

Market Researchers

The excellent reputation of our market research staff has led to a number of demands from exporters. In addition, a number of our customers—as has been our custom—are using this service more and more. As a result, our RFRs have increased by more than 150 percent in the past two years. The staff has virtually no time available to itself, and, in fact, has been averaging more than ten hours per week overtime per individual staff member for the last six months. This workload not only endangers the quality of service provided, but also undercuts the creativity of the workers in this area. Assistance here is desperately needed.

Administrative Staff Assistants

We presently have one and one-half assistants working with 300 customers and 20 field personnel. Because of this heavy workload, our reply rate averages 14 days. Needless to say, this rate is embarrassingly slow. The addition of the field personnel and the market researchers can only make this situation worse.

Please contact me by the beginning of next week if you agree with these requests and plan to grant them. This would enable me to set in motion the proper administrative processes.

Sincerely,

APPENDIX B

CIRCUITOUS ILLUSTRATIONS

As we have said repeatedly throughout this text, the decision to bottom-line or not to bottom-line ultimately rests with you, the writer. In the vast majority of instances we recommend that you do so. But there are special sensitive cases that call for the tact and diplomacy of a circuitous organizational pattern.

To help you when such occasions arise, we include nine illustrations of various circuitous patterns. These examples are divided into two sections, the first dealing with negative information situations, and the second dealing with negative persuasive requests. Each example could serve as a prototype for various circumstances.

CIRCUITOUS PERSUASIVE MESSAGES

Message A

This letter gives the initial impression of being bottom-lined. It immediately begins with the subject and then summarizes the attached proposal. But what is the real bottom line? What does the writer really want?

That answer can be found at the beginning of the last paragraph. The writer wants to demonstrate the proposed products to the reader and to the reader's staff!

Two aspects of this message deserve special attention:

1. The writer avoids sounding like a huckster by dealing with content rather than superficialities.
2. The writer first offers a specific analysis of the school's needs and then documents the company's expertise in these areas.

Bottom-line rules applied:

> BOTTOM-LINE RULE 10: IN PERSUASIVE SITUATIONS, WHERE YOU DO NOT KNOW HOW YOUR READER WILL REACT TO WHAT YOU ASK FOR, BOTTOM-LINE YOUR REQUEST IN ALL CASES EXCEPT:
>
> 1. THOSE IN WHICH YOU DON'T (OR BARELY) KNOW THE READER, AND TO ASK SOMETHING IMMEDIATELY OF A RELATIVE (OR ABSOLUTE) STRANGER WOULD PROBABLY BE PERCEIVED AS PUSHY.
> 2. THOSE IN WHICH THE RELATIONSHIP BETWEEN YOU AND YOUR READER IS NOT CLOSE OR WARM.
>
> BOTTOM-LINE RULE 13: USE A CIRCUITOUS ORGANIZATIONAL PATTERN IN NEGATIVE REQUESTS WRITTEN TO PERSONS IN HIGHER POWER POSITIONS, BUT STILL HIGH-IMPACT YOUR ACTION REQUEST.

June 18, 19—

Susan Jones
United States College
51 Elm Street
Trenton, NJ 08769

Dear Ms. Jones:

There are two issues that need to be addressed in the area of word processing at United States College:

1. How can immediate word processing requirements be satisfied?
2. How can word processing and data processing be integrated to meet the college's future requirements for information processing?

The attached proposal addresses some of the major requirements that XYZ feels are critical to United States' integrated information network. In addition, the proposal details the current status of the Statement of Opinion, an independent advisory report comparing how XYZ and other word processing firms have fulfilled their commitment to providing products that fit within an integrated network approach. As you will see, XYZ leads in a vast majority of categories.

We feel that XYZ can provide the college with products that meet the college's immediate needs. In addition, XYZ's performance in fulfilling its contractual obligations demonstrates that today's products will have the ability to meet the college's future information-processing requirements.

We would welcome the opportunity to demonstrate the proposed products to you and your staff. If you have any questions pertaining to this proposal, please give me a call.

Message B

After a brief pleasantry, this message moves immediately to a contract sentence—we need your input and decision to establish clear objectives and proceed with the simulation study. The contract sentence shows the general direction of the letter and alludes to the letter's purpose, but the actual statement of purpose does not appear until the final paragraph when the writer asks for approval of the study.

The key point to note in this letter is that because the writer begins with a contract sentence, the reader is not blindsided by the action request. It is true that to make a valid judgment of the objectives the writer will have to reread the entire letter, but at least the reader is not caught off-guard by the ending request.

Bottom-line rules applied:

BOTTOM-LINE RULE 7: NEVER KEEP SECRET FROM THE READER (OR YOURSELF) THE DIRECTION(S) IN WHICH A COMPLICATED ANALYTICAL DISCUSSION WILL GO. MAKE A

CONTRACT WITH YOUR READERS AND FULFILL EVERY CLAUSE OF THAT CONTRACT, IN THE SAME SEQUENTIAL ORDER AS CONTRACTED.

BOTTOM-LINE RULE 13: USE A CIRCUITOUS ORGANIZATIONAL PATTERN IN NEGATIVE REQUESTS WRITTEN TO PERSONS IN HIGHER POWER POSITIONS, BUT STILL HIGH-IMPACT YOUR ACTION REQUEST.

John Edmond
Director of Information Services
General Hospital

Dear John,

I want to thank you and your staff for the time you have spent with me during the last three months working on the Hospital Information System. However, in order to establish clear objectives for the simulation study and to proceed with it, we now need your input and decisions.

At the meeting with your staff on September 11, 19—, I presented a brief on the idea simulation, the methodology involved, and the various simulators that are available on the terminal network.

The following issues were selected to be studied:

1. The capabilities of your present system to handle the additional workload you expect to add during the next year.
2. The simulation tools to be used.
3. The manpower needs to add to the study at a later date.
4. The targeted completion date (November 30, 19—).

I would appreciate your reviewing the above issues and giving us input about them. Then please give your approval to the simulation study so that your staff and I may proceed with it. This project has a lot of potential, and we hope to tap it as quickly as possible.

Message C

Here is a totally circuitous request. The writer withholds her purpose until the last paragraph. Until that point she extends courtesies, offers appreciation, and names areas she would like to study further. In essence, she makes her case and then states her request.

Note, however, that the writer states the request in a clear, straightforward manner. As a result, the reader should have no problem determining what the writer wants.

Bottom-line rules applied:

BOTTOM-LINE RULE 4:	ALWAYS HIGH-IMPACT AN ACTION REQUEST AND BOTTOM-LINE IT IF APPROPRIATE.
BOTTOM-LINE RULE 10:	IN PERSUASIVE SITUATIONS, WHERE YOU DO NOT KNOW HOW YOUR READER WILL REACT TO WHAT YOU ASK FOR, BOTTOM-LINE YOUR REQUEST IN ALL CASES EXCEPT:
	1. THOSE IN WHICH YOU DON'T (OR BARELY) KNOW THE READER, AND TO ASK SOMETHING IMMEDIATELY OF A RELATIVE (OR ABSOLUTE) STRANGER WOULD PROBABLY BE PERCEIVED AS PUSHY.
	2. THOSE IN WHICH THE RELATIONSHIP BETWEEN YOU AND YOUR READER IS NOT CLOSE OR WARM.
BOTTOM-LINE RULE 13:	USE A CIRCUITOUS ORGANIZATIONAL PATTERN IN NEGATIVE REQUESTS WRITTEN TO PERSONS IN HIGHER POWER POSITIONS, BUT STILL HIGH-IMPACT YOUR ACTION REQUEST.

Gordon Richards
Vice-President of Data Processing
ABCD Company
San Francisco, CA 35498

Dear Mr. Richards:

Thank you for taking time out of your busy schedule to talk to me yesterday. Even though we discussed a wide range of topics, I think I gained a good insight into the operation and services of the ABCD Company's Data Processing Department.

More specifically, I believe there are several areas within your department that I would like to explore with you in greater detail:

1. Application programmer productivity.
2. Improved response time to terminal users.
3. Efficient space utilization.
4. End-user education.

My prior experience working with other customers in ABCD's industry can make a valuable contribution to the continued success of your department.

Mr. Richards, with your permission I would like to stop by ABCD next Wednesday afternoon to talk to your Manager of Application Development. I will call you early next week to learn if you approve this meeting. I look forward to working closely with you and other ABCD professionals.

Sincerely,

Jane Jones

Message D

This writer begins by offering a historical perspective on the Control Information System (CIS). In the third paragraph the writer begins to make a specific case for the request. Then, in the fourth paragraph, the writer makes the request.

The persuasive approach used in this memo is highly risky. From one perspective, the opening is confusing—the reader may ask, "Why are you telling me this?"—and risks being insulting. "I already know this!" the reader may claim. As a result the reader may stop reading before arriving at the request.

From another perspective, the request is embedded near the middle of the message. As a result, if the reader begins skimming the message, there is a good chance he or she will overlook the specific request.

Such an approach should therefore be used only in situations where the reader is likely to have strong negative feelings toward the request.

Bottom-line rules applied:

```
BOTTOM-LINE RULE 10: IN PERSUASIVE SITUATIONS,
                     WHERE YOU DO NOT KNOW
                     HOW YOUR READER WILL RE-
                     ACT TO WHAT YOU ASK FOR,
                     BOTTOM-LINE YOUR REQUEST
                     IN ALL CASES EXCEPT:
```

1. THOSE IN WHICH YOU DON'T (OR BARELY) KNOW THE READER, AND TO ASK SOMETHING IMMEDIATELY OF A RELATIVE (OR ABSOLUTE) STRANGER WOULD PROBABLY BE PERCEIVED AS PUSHY.

2. THOSE IN WHICH THE RELATIONSHIP BETWEEN YOU AND YOUR READER IS NOT CLOSE OR WARM.

BOTTOM-LINE RULE 13: USE A CIRCUITOUS ORGANIZATIONAL PATTERN IN NEGATIVE REQUESTS WRITTEN TO PERSONS IN HIGHER POWER POSITIONS, BUT STILL HIGH-IMPACT YOUR ACTION REQUEST.

April 15, 19—

TO:

FROM:

SUBJECT: Control Information System

Control Information System (CIS) was implemented in XYZ in July 19—, and is presently employed by all XYZ operating companies. CIS provides maintenance time values by product. It utilizes a sampling approach in the selection of craftpersons who report actual maintenance data by product. The system accumulates these data in a centralized base with the ability to provide outputs on demand. Some output reports provided are station products, access line, and travel per service order summaries.

CIS also is used as a vehicle to document maintenance hours charged. Had the CIS sampling method not been acceptable, all personnel would have been required to report data on a daily basis.

The transfer of craft personnel from Business Services to the Distribution segment has made it essential that we enlist the services of your department in providing CIS information to all personnel. This is the only way we can maintain the validity of the data collected.

I am requesting authorization to conduct training sessions for these (approximately 2 percent) randomly selected craftpersons transferring to Distribution so that we may continue to provide this information.

Training classes last approximately 6–8 hours and are charged to an unmeasured code (see attachment). Selected personnel are normally required to participate in the study for six months.

Mr. Jones of your staff is familiar with this situation.

Questions concerning this matter may be directed to Ms. Smith or Ms. Hopkins of my staff.

Attachment

CIRCUITOUS NEGATIVE MESSAGES

Message A

Here is a conventional bad-news letter. The bad news is framed by positive statements and pleasantries but is delivered in a clear, efficient manner. There is therefore little chance that the reader will misunderstand the message's content.

Bottom-line rules applied:

BOTTOM-LINE RULE 12: THINK TWICE BEFORE USING A DIRECT APPROACH IN NEGATIVE MESSAGES UPWARD.

BOTTOM-LINE RULE 13: USE A CIRCUITOUS ORGANIZATIONAL PATTERN IN NEGATIVE REQUESTS WRITTEN TO PERSONS IN HIGHER POWER POSITIONS, BUT STILL HIGH-IMPACT YOUR ACTION REQUEST.

Dear Mr. Atkins:

Attached is our report on the Sound Level Survey conducted by Mr. Jemison at your facility on November 1. We are extremely pleased to have been able to assist you in your efforts to monitor the noise level within your firm. And we commend you for your interest in the safety and health of your employees.

The results of the survey indicate there are three areas in the company that are over 90 DBA. The areas are metallic fabrications, cold draw, and segmentation. Recommendations listed at the end of this report should help reduce noise levels in these areas.

I personally thank you for your cooperation during the survey. If you have any questions, or if we may be of any further assistance, please feel free to call upon us.

Sincerely,

Bill Jones
Industrial Safety & Health Section

Message B

The writer here chooses a straightforward, aggressive style, but blunts some of the directness by using a circuitous organizational pattern. The reader already knows the writer's feelings on this topic, so any other approach would be either too aggressive (a direct organizational pattern) or too transparent (a less direct style).

Bottom-line rules applied:

BOTTOM-LINE RULE 12: THINK TWICE BEFORE USING A DIRECT APPROACH IN NEGA-TIVE MESSAGES UPWARD.

BOTTOM-LINE RULE 13: USE A CIRCUITOUS ORGANIZA-TIONAL PATTERN IN NEGATIVE REQUESTS WRITTEN TO PER-SONS IN HIGHER POWER POSI-TIONS, BUT STILL HIGH-IMPACT YOUR ACTION REQUEST.

BUMCO MINING

Charles Ferris
Washington, D.C.

Dear Chuck:

On several occasions we have discussed the improper manner in which the U.S. Government Coal Tracts in West Virginia have been delineated and proposed for bidding. Surface mine tracts were delineated by grouping blocks of U.S. government ownership, with minimal consideration of coal outcrops or neighboring property owners. The problem is considerably worsened in the underground tracts because deep mining is relatively inflexible. It is necessary to control 10 to 15 continuous square miles of unobstructed mineral ownership to begin a new deep mine.

The Athens and Oxford Springs tracts are prime examples of the problem. If they are made available for public sealed bid in December 19—, it opens the possibility that these tracts will be acquired by someone who cannot develop them. If this happens, the government will not collect the revenues it expects, and we will not be able to proceed with plans for new mines.

Below is a list of specific reasons why the Athens and Oxford Springs tracts should not be placed in a sealed bid situation.

1. Sixty percent of the delineated Athens tract and 25 percent of the Oxford Springs tract are controlled by an established mining company having the reserves and resources necessary to convert them into operating mines (see attached maps).
2. Both of these tracts are highly intermixed with coal ownership we control. In order to open an underground mine in these two areas, it is necessary to control 10 to 15 square miles of continuous ownership. We cannot accomplish this without government help in this area.
3. Both of these tracts are subdivided by a major fault that makes it impractical to locate a true "Logical Mining Unit" within either tract.
4. Our company has made a long-term commitment to mines in the area. We would be greatly damaged by speculators.
5. Bids in competition with BUMCO on these two tracts will be strictly speculative in nature. Such bidding would violate the regulations that were, in part, written to avoid undue speculation. The closed-bid system actually encourages speculation.
6. BUMCO cannot afford to pay ransom to speculators. If speculation is allowed to continue, it will destroy our mining plans.

I therefore suggest that an outside contractor make a reasonable assessment of the bid value of Athens and Oxford Springs and then allow BUMCO to secure a lease for that amount. The only other reasonable alternative is to allow open bidding on the property.

Chuck, I look forward to your comments.

Message C

Here is another example of how to offer background before the recommendations. Such an approach should be used only when the reader will be inclined *not* to be willing to grant the recommendation. *Note:* Before reading this memo, the reader thought that the writer had finished preparing for this bid.

April 16, 19—

TO: Superior

FROM: Subordinate

While I was in XYZ Oil's Denver office on March 30 and 31 to review federal leasing procedures, I had an opportunity to meet and talk with numerous petroleum personnel. Some of these were:

Jack Harris, General Manager of Field Engineering
Mark Giles, Manager of Engineering Construction
Stan Painter, Vice-President of Engineering Research
Dave Collins, Land Agent—Law
Joe Bonner, Land Agent—Research

The land agents briefed me on the recent leasing history in Colorado and Wyoming; they stated that all leasing to date has been by sealed bid. The attached summary from Dave Collins, ABCD, shows bonus prices in total dollars, dollars per acre, and dollars per gallon. You can see that successful bid bonuses have ranged from — to — dollars per gallon in sealed bidding, and they could go considerably higher at oral auctions.

Joe Bonner has been extensively researching ownership in the West Hill Tract and has recognized a need to finish the title search on the tract. This entails spending $2,000 to $3,000 in identifying mineral rights owners so we can begin expanding the boundaries of the tract as soon as possible. He feels it may be advantageous to bid for the Shady Acres Church Tract in the West Bendix area in June.

On March 31, I attended the South Fork Regional Oil Team meeting, which was held to receive public and industry comments on planned leasing activities and to establish land use priorities in the area. At the meeting, a lease sale notice for April 30, 19—, was released. A detailed notice, with a copy of the draft lease, will be available in a few days.

In order to be thoroughly prepared for that Wyoming Oil lease sale in June, I make the following recommendations:

1. Designate a team to fully research and digest every legal and technical aspect of federal leasing and then develop a strategy for bidding. The team members will:
   a. Coordinate lease preparation and strategy, and keep ABCD and XYZ informed.
   b. Determine tract tonnages and geology.
   c. Comply with all details of the law, including making all payments and filing reports.
   d. Research and correct all federal land and leasing errors (12-acre dual assessment with U.S.A., 40 acres currently leased by ABCD being offered for lease again, acreage count errors by ABC/DEF).

2. Draft a schedule of activities, through June 30, 19—, to coordinate leasing efforts.
3. Respond to the recent request for information on tracts in which we are interested.
4. Determine maximum value of the West Hill Tract.
5. Send a representative to the April 30 Denver lease sale to examine bid procedures.
5. Arrange to have all fees and 20 percent of the cash bonus payments on hand for disbursement on the sale day.

If you agree with my recommendations, I will need your assistance in assembling the lease team.

Attachment

Message D

In this situation the reader initially requested a sample text. The writer, in turn, refuses the request and offers another. Notice how the writer:

1. Begins on a pleasant note.
2. Gives reasons why the initial text is unsuitable.
3. Offers a discount if the reader wants to purchase the text.
4. Substitutes and subtly sells the second text.
5. Gives the reader a copy of the second text.

Dear Mr. Hall:

Thank you for your recent letter requesting a copy of *Psychology and Linguistics* by Jane and John Doe. I am pleased to see people in managerial development becoming interested in ABCD's texts.

I am quite familiar with the Does' text, so I'd like to summarize it for you. *Psychology and Linguistics* is really a psycholinguistics text that fully integrates psychology and linguistics. This highly technical text focuses on the three processes basic to language use—listening (comprehension of speech), speaking (production of speech), and acquisition of these abilities by children.

As you can see, this text would not meet your training needs. This 608-page hardbound text sells for $19.95, although I can arrange a 20 percent professional discount if you want to purchase a personal copy.

A text that might better satisfy your needs is the fourth edition of the now classic *Language in Business* by I. S. Jones. If you start reading this book you will find it difficult to put down. Jones uses the principles of modern semantics to show how that understanding can be applied to everyday life.

Through an examination of the different uses of language, he shows us the crucial role of language in managerial affairs and dire possibilities inherent in the misuse of language. I highly recommend this book as supplementary text for your managerial communication module. In paperback, *Language in Business* sells for $6.95 and has 318 pages.

I have already asked the shipping department to send you a complimentary copy of Jones's text. You should find the book fascinating and useful. Good luck in your upcoming training session.

Message E

Here is another classic bad-news letter. Notice, again, how the letter:

1. Begins pleasantly.
2. Offers reasons for the refusal.
3. Subordinates the refusal.
4. Ends on a pleasant, agreeable note.

Dear Mr. Patrick:

Thank you for your letter of September 23. Like the union, the management of ABCD Rubber is sincerely concerned about worker safety. No other area is as important. We were especially proud of the Akron plant's recent safety commendation from OSHA.

Decisions about budget allocations are always difficult to make. This year's allocations have shown our concern with the environment in which our employees live and work. We have put more than $2.5 million into pollution control equipment for the Akron plant.

Akron's overall safety record was one of the primary reasons we decided to concentrate funds in pollution control. Although we are deeply concerned about last year's injuries, we feel that these injuries were the exception rather than the rule.

In terms of the big picture, the three-year safety record of the Akron plant is markedly better than the national average for plants of this type. One reason for this enviable record is our continued dedication to safety, as evidenced by an average 25 percent per year increase in the Akron safety budget over the last three years. Therefore, while I cannot grant your request to increase our safety budget by 50 percent, I can assure you of our continued concern with and dedication to the safety of our Akron workers.

Jim, no industrial firm in America today is as committed to worker safety as ABCD. We will take all reasonable steps necessary to protect our workers. Please convey this dedication to all of our friends at the Akron plant.

Sincerely,

INDEX

A

Action request:
  bottom-line if appropriate, 35
  burying, 35
  come right out with it, 36
  high-impact, 35, 38, 66, 101
  look like checklists, 38
  managers, 36
  negative persuasive, 66, 68, 69
  numerous actions requested, 38
  risk-taker, 36
  subordinates, 36
  training sessions, 36
  written upward in organization, 36
Anxiety, 99
Appendix, information:
  detailed, not read in entirety, 39,
    86, 101
  dubious utility, 39, 101
  illustrations, 104, 105-149
    bottom-line, 104, 105-135
    circuitous, 104, 136-149
  questionable importance, 39, 101
Assumptions, avoid, 24-27, 28
Audiovisual equipment, 98

B

Backsliding:
  bottom-lining only one of
    purposes, 28-30

briefing before purpose, 31-32
  evidences, 28, 35
Bad news, 57, 61
Benefits, product, 55, 56
Blind/persuasive messages:
  circuitous pattern, 50, 55
  cold calls, 55, 56, 57
  direct mail, 55, 57
  dramatize benefits of product, 55
  reader's mind conditioned, 55
  ritual, 55
  rivet attention on product, 55
  sales proposal, 55-56
  we know little about readers, 55
  when, 55
Bottom-lining:
  action request, 35-38 (see also
    Action request)
  appendix, 39-40
  assumptions to avoid, 24-27
  clinic, 95-104 (see also Clinic)
  complex communications, 41-46
  illustrations, 105-135
  mastering the mind set, 71-93
  memos, 18-20
  negative messages, 50, 57-59,
    60-69, 87, 102, 120-126,
    136-143, 143-149
  nonsensitive messages, 17-46
  order of importance to reader,
    38-39
  positive messages, 51-59
  recognize bottom-line sentences,
    73-82 (see also Recognition of
    bottom-line)

Bottom-Lining *(cont'd.)*
relapses, 28-40
relationship, position, message,
49-50
rules listed, 102-103
save reader's time, 21-23
sensitive messages, 47-69
"So what?" factor, 73-82
what to tell readers, 17-18
what your purpose is, 18
what you want them to do, 18
why you are writing, 17
writing first draft messages, 83-93
Breakout room, 99
Briefings, 28, 31-34, 102, 107,
115-116, 117, 120, 125

C

Circuitous pattern:
blind/persuasive messages, 50, 55
fear being forthright, 50
negative messages—up, 50, 60-66,
103, 143-149
negative persuasive messages, 50,
66-69, 136-143
risk, 90, 93
Clinic:
actual operation, 98-99
after concept grasped, 99
analysis of memos, letters, etc., 98
appendix illustrations, 104
before first meeting, 99
bottom-line rules, 102
breakout room, 99
comparison of beginnings, 99
coordinator, 98, 100
credo, 100
definition, 98
equipment, 98
fellow workers meet, 98
guidelines, 97-101
how writers place ideas, 98
insecurity, not thoroughness,
99-101
messages selected for analysis, 98
myths, 99-100

organizational patterns discussed,
99
pledges, 100-101
small work groups, 99
spread the word, 98
this book read, 99
transparencies of each memo, 98
what you need to operate, 98-99
when writers place ideas, 98
where writers place ideas, 98
why people fail to bottom-line, 99
willing colleagues, 98
wrapup, 99
Coherence, 84
Cold calls, 55, 56, 57
Complex communications (*see*
Reports)
Conclusion:
give first, 27
negative messages—up, 65
Contract sentence:
after bottom-line sentence, 42
beginning of subsections, 42
bottom line, 45
definitions, 42
examples, 42
for each subsection, 45
guiding, 42
longer, complex documents, 42
organizes, 42, 43
sequence of factors, 42, 43
specifies what will be discussed, 44,
45
transition, 45, 46
Coordinator, clinic, 98, 100
Corrections, 65
Cover letter, 55-56
Credo, 100

D

Defense of conclusion, 27
Detail, extreme, 65
Direct mail, 55, 57
Direct pattern, 50
Draft, final, 27

E

Efficiency, 81-82
Emotional reactions, 49
Equipment, clinic, 98
Explanation, 58, 61

F

Final draft, 27
First draft:
  coherence, 84
  forethought, 84
  key, 83
  organize before writing, 84
  review your notes, 85
  sensitive situations, 87-93
    blunt the impact, 90
    circuitous pattern, risk, 90, 93
    how reader will react, 87
    negative messages, 87-90
    power relationship with reader,
      87
    practice cases, 87-90
    writing down, 91-93
  thinking *before* you write, 83, 84, 85
  what is bottom line, 85, 88
  what you are going to do, 84
  where to place bottom line, 86, 87
  why you are writing, 83

G

Good news, 51, 103

I

Identification (*see* Recognition of
    bottom line)
Illustrations:
  bottom-line, 105-135
  circuitous, 136-149

Information:
  detailed, not read in entirety, 39,
      86, 101
  dubious utility, 39, 102
  nonsensitive, 15-46 (*see also*
      Nonsensitive messages)
  order of importance to reader,
      38-39
  organizing, 38
  questionable importance, 39, 102
Informational messages, 50, 105-113
Insecurity, 99-101

J

Justification of conclusion, 27

K

Key word, 29

M

Mailing lists, 55
Market research, 55
Memos:
  briefings, 31-34
  examine your own, 20
  money saved, 20
  more than one purpose, 28-29
  needlessly discursive, 19
  non-bottom-lined, 18-20
  potentially useless information, 20
  relevance to you, 20
  searching for bottom line, 19
  two transparencies of each, 98
  typical, 18-19
  unsolicited, 74-77
  wading through, 20
  wasting time, 18-20
  writers in your organization, 20
Messages:
  assumptions to avoid, 24-27
  blind/persuasive, 50, 55-57

Messages *(cont'd.)*
  bottom line or not, 49
  bottom line to save time, 21-23
  circuitous negative, 50, 60-66, 103,
    143-149
  circuitous persuasive, 50, 66-69,
    136-143
  contract sentences (*see* Contract
    sentences)
  first draft, 83-93
  informational, 50, 105-113
  negative, 50, 57-59, 60-66, 66-69,
    87, 103, 120-126, 136-143,
    143-149
  negative/persuasive, 50, 66-69,
    136-143
  non-bottom-lined, 18-20
  nonsensitive, 15-46
  positive, 50, 51-52, 113-119
  positive/persuasive, 50, 53-54,
    126-135
  pushy, 53
  relapses to avoid, 28, 35
  sensitive, 47-69
  subject, 25
  writer fears being forthright, 50
Mind-set:
  first-draft messages, 83-93
  recognize bottom-line sentences,
    73-82
Myths, 99-100

N

Negative messages—down:
  adaptation to reader, 58
  bad news, 57
  direct pattern, 50, 58-59
  don't be overbearing, 57
  explanation, 58
  how to bottom-line, 120-126
  kudos for reader, 58
  message presented, 58
  not wishy-washy, 57
  stress your honesty, 57
  stress your straightforwardness,
    57-58
  style of writing, 58

  subordinate expects orders, 57
  unless extenuating circumstances,
    57
  you *are* the boss, 57
Negative messages—up:
  avoid appearing transparent, 62
  basic sentence structure, 65
  bottom-lining can be suicidal, 61
  circuitous pattern, 50, 60-66,
    66-69, 103, 143-149
  conclusions, 65
  create distance, 65
  difficult situations, 61
  explanations of reasons, 61
  extreme detail, 65
  get-off-subject ending, 61
  longer version, 64-65
  low-impact terms, 61
  padding needed, 63
  personal and impersonal, 65
  pleasant beginning, 61
  relationship with boss, 61
  special consideration, 87
  suggestions, 65
  too blunt or curt, 61, 63
Negative persuasive messages:
  approach gingerly, 66
  circuitous pattern, 50, 66-69,
    136-143
  high-impact action request, 66, 68,
    69
  not bottom-line, 67
Non-sensitive messages:
  assumptions to avoid, 24-27
  complex communications, 41-46
  memos, 17-20
  95 percent of business writing, 17
  relapse into not bottom-lining,
    28-40
  save reader's time, 21-23
Notes, review, 85

O

Orders, 57
Organizational patterns:
  blind/persuasive messages, 50
  circuitous, 50

clear at beginning, 41
complex communications, 41, 46
determine before writing, 84
direct (bottom-lined), 50
information-conveying message, 50
negative messages, 50
negative/persuasive messages, 50
never force reader to infer, 46
ones used, 99
positive messages, 50
positive/persuasive messages, 50
preferable for you, 50
sensitive messages, 49-50
writer fears being forthright, 50
Overhead projectors, 98

P

Patterns, organizational (*see*
  Organizational patterns)
Persuasive messages, 55-57, 103,
  126-135, 136-143(*see also* Positive
  persuasive messages, Negative
  persuasive messages)
Pledges, 100-101
Positions, power, 49
Positive messages, 50, 51-52, 113-119
Positive/persuasive messages, 50,
  53-54, 126-135
Power positions, 49
Problem, 56
Product, selling, 55-56
Projectors, 98
Purpose:
  assuming readers know, 25
  briefing, 31-34, 102
  buried, 29
  mandatory, 32
  more than one, 28, 102
  not same as subject, 25-26
  reasons for not stating first, 22
  stating first, 18, 22, 23, 28, 31, 102

R

Recognition of bottom line:
  before you write, 81-82

efficiency, 81-82
likely responses, 74-75
longer passages, 77-81
managers had problems, 74
message's purpose, 75
non-bottom-line beginning, 74-75
practice, 74-81
professional obfuscators, 78
reader responses to revisions, 75
revised bottom-line beginnings, 75
significance of message, 75
"So what?" factor, 74-77
training classes, 74
unsolicited memo or letter, 74, 75
writers need to be able, 74
Recommendation, 27
Relationship, reader and writer,
  49,50
Reports:
  complex, multisectioned, 41, 45
  contract sentence, 42-46 (*see also*
    Contract sentence)
  direction of discussion, 42, 44, 45
  logical skeletal framework, 41, 42,
    44
  many bottom-line statements, 41
  more complicated, 44
  organizational pattern, 41, 46
  sequence of factors, 42, 43
  subsections, 41, 42, 45
    bottom line, 45
    contract sentence for each, 42,
      45
    each has bottom line, 41, 45
    multisection report, 41
    specify topics, 45
    state purpose, 41
    tell how organized, 41
    very complicated report, 45
  synopsis, 45
  transitions, 45, 46
Requests, positive persuasive, 53-54

S

Sales proposal, 55-56
Scientific papers, 56
Selling, effective, 55,56

Sensitive messages:
  blind persuasive situations, 55-57
  first drafts, 87-90
  good news, 51-52
  negative, 57-59, 60-66, 66-69
    downward, 57-59
    persuasive, 66-69
    upward, 60-66
  positive, 51-52
  positive persuasive requests, 53
  relationship, position, message,
    49-50
"So what?" factor:
  effective, 74
  efficiency, 81-82
  longer passages, 77-81
  message's purpose, 75
  practice, 74-81
  training classes, 74
  unsolicited memo or letter, 74-77
Subject, not same as purpose, 25-26
Subordinates, 57
Suggestions, corrections, 65

T

Thinking, *before* you write, 83, 84, 85
Thoroughness, 99-101
Time:
  saving, 21-23
  stating purpose first, 18, 22, 23
  wasting, 18-20
Transitional contract sentences, 45,
    46
Transparencies, memos, 98

W

Word, key, 29
Work groups, clinic, 99
Writing:
  final draft, 27
  first drafts, 83-93